LOST GARDENS
OF
ESSEX

Wendy Stubbings

Ian Henry Publications

ISBN 0 86025 525 5

The picture on the front cover is a detail from
A Prospect of Weald Hall in the County of Essex
Oil on canvas attributed to
William Van Der Hagen
(Courtesy of Sotheby's)

Published by
Ian Henry Publications, Ltd.
20 Park Drive, Romford, Essex RM1 4LH
and printed by
Gomer Press, Llandysul, Ceredigion SA44 4QL

Introduction

The text and illustrations of this book are a compilation of the sources available wholly from the Essex Record Office. There is plenty of material available for such research from many other sources. The Garden History Society is now doing much research, but for my purposes of a general and interesting study, I had enough material to produce, I hope, a readable and informative study into many of our lost gardens of Essex.

Essex in recent times has had a bad press and one would certainly not think of Essex in terms of grand gardens, unlike the County of Cornwall, although today it can boast a Royal Horticultural Society garden at Hyde Hall, Rettendon; a wonderful hilltop site started by Dr. and Mrs. Robinson and contains amongst many other wonderful plants, the national collections of Viburnum and Malus. Here is Beth Chatto's garden at Elmstead Market, based on ecological ideas with separate areas that cater for sun-loving plants through to bog plants; she also has an extensive nursery of unusual plants. Essex is also the home of Hugh Johnson, 'Tradescant' of the R.H.S. Journal, who gardens at Saling Hall. During the summer months there are many beautiful gardens, both large and small that are open for visitors under the National Garden Scheme.

This book is about the wonderful gardens that have been lost; during the 18th century, Essex could boast some of the grandest houses and gardens in the country. Most of the houses have long since gone, many under new developments, especially where the London Boroughs have encroached into Essex. Some gardens may still be there, but their beauty has diminished. Many an 18th century landscape can still be seen, where open spaces remain; and a number have been turned into Country Parks and wildlife areas of conservation.

Essex can be justly proud of its horticultural associations; many of the names synonymous with garden design or plant collectors will appear on the ensuing pages, but one mention must be made of a man that will not appear under the gardening élite, as he did not own or design a garden, but was our first botanist, that is John Ray. Many think it should have been Ray and not Carl von Linné who had the credit for the classification of plants. John Ray was born in 1627 at Black Notley, the son of the village blacksmith, and educated at Braintree School and Trinity College, Cambridge. After lecturing on Greek and mathematics and taking orders, his passion for nature took him through the British Isles and on the Continent. He worked out the Latin system of plant classification that was later perfected by Linné. The last twenty-six years of his life were spent in Essex: he died in 1705.

Essex was also the producer of at least two apple species. The D'Arcy Spice apple was first found in the garden of the Hall at Tolleshunt D'Arcy in 1785. It is in season from December to April and has a patchy russet skin with a sweet spicy flavour. Another less well-known apple was the Chelmsford Wonder, a cooking apple, rarely seen these days.

Once the prerogative of the rich, gardening now is the passionate pastime of the masses. Television series, magazines, garden centres and nurseries abound;

and an overwhelming interest has arisen in garden visiting.

Between 1984 and 1988 English Heritage published 44 volumes of the Registers of Parks and Gardens, listing all properties of antiquity, historical association or aesthetic merit that should be hopefully preserved. The Essex Garden Trust was started in 1996; not only does it wish to record all historical gardens, but to rescue 'lost' gardens, and to stimulate interest in creating new plating schemes for urban areas and suchlike.

An interesting quote from Hugh Johnson probably sums up why the British have an overwhelming passion for their gardens: 'There is a perplexing paradox in the fact that Britain has one of the poorest natural flora of the temperate world, yet certainly the richest range of imported plants growing in their gardens. Our countryside is very simple; our gardens the most complex on earth' ['The Origins of Plants No. 1 - The Seeds of Adventure' in Telegraph Sunday Magazine, 17 May, 1981].

I hope the ensuing text and illustrations will give an insight into the 'lost' gardens of Essex and to make one look closer into the landscape to see what can be salvaged from the past.

Gidea Hall, near Romford, about 1730 (from an engraving by Humphry Repton)

Chapter One

The Early Years

It cannot be said when gardening began for pleasure, unless we regard Francis Bacon's statement that "God Almighty first planted a garden" as a horticultural fact. Indeed the first gardens we do know of are religious; the monasteries all had their gardens, which were used for medicinal and culinary purposes, and as will be seen in the ensuing text some of these monasteries became the grand country houses with their marvellous gardens, after the reformation. There were sacristy gardens attached to churches and abbeys that would have included lilies, holly and ivy for Christmas, palms for Palm Sunday, roses for Corpus Christi and sweet herbs for strewing. These were the origins of the formal flower gardens; our magnificent parkland has its origins in the medieval deer parks. Essex had 102 deer parks in the greatest period between 1200 and 1350. They were created by the surplus wealth landowners were receiving from the increased agricultural development following the deforestation during this period. The feudal services of their tenants provided plenty of labour. Layer Marney was an early example when William Marney was granted licence to impark in 1264. Weald Hall was probably created as a deer park in the 12th century, as part of the estate of Waltham Abbey, and no doubt the monks, less pious than nowadays, would have enjoyed hunting and eating deer. This period would have been the beginning of the landscape as we now see it. The parks were enclosed by a wooden fence or 'pale' on a high boundary bank, many of these can still be seen in old woodland. Danbury Park was laid out about 1290, the three existing lakes were formed at this time. In the 1880s a large old oak was felled, and a small silver coin of the reign of King John was found embedded in it. William de Montchesy [d.1289], lord of the manor of Great Braxted, had a warren made there, and by 1342 a deer park existed. Leez Priory gained a licence to enclose 100 acres in 1381 to make into a park. Sir Thomas Cooke [d.1478] of Gidea Hall had a licence to impark 180 acres in 1466. After 1350 the hunting parks declined because of lack of labour due to the plagues of the second half of the 14th century. There was further disparkment between 1500-1640 when the growth of population demanded more agricultural lands. John Norden's map of Essex, 1594, shows 50 parks, and by 1696 there were only 24 according to John Oliver's map of Essex.

During the 16th century gardens were steadily emerging from the medieval hortus conclusus, the protected enclosures where productivity and visual beauty combined in unambitious and largely anonymous simplicity. Civil peace returned to England during the reign of Henry VII and it was no longer necessary to have fortified houses, people were looking to the wider horizon. They were travelling abroad, first as hunters and adventurers, followed by traders and botanists. Gardening became fashionable, influenced by the Italians and French. The Huguenots had a great influence on gardening when they fled to this country in the 1540s and again after Saint Bartholomew's night in 1572.

It was as early as this that the first plants were being imported from Turkey such as tulips, anemones and crown imperial fritillarias. The 16th century also saw the printing of the first gardening books, although there are four known Anglo-Saxon herbals surviving, one of which is a translation of the Herbarium of Apuleius Platonicus that probably dates from the time of the Norman Conquest. The first herbal to be printed in England dates from 1525 the so-called Bankes Herbell that was superseded the following year by The Grete Herball. The first important botanical work in English was William Turner's A New Herball of 1551-68. Thomas Tusser, who was born in Rivenhall and farmed in the Stour valley, in 1557 published his Five Hundred Good Points of Husbandry, illustrating the everyday life of the Elizabethan and many of the lists of vegetables and herbs are the same as we still grow today; there were 42 herbs for kitchen use and another 23 for salads and sauces. Under Herbs and Roots to boil and butter he lists: beans, carrots, cabbages, parsnips, rape, turnip, peas, pumpkins, radishes, gourds and 'citrons' as well as over 20 fruits and nuts. The last known of the 16th century English herbals is John Gerard's The Herball or General Historie of Plantes of 1597. He was a barber-surgeon, but his interest in plants led him to become the superintendent of the garden of Lord Burghley in the Strand.

One Essex garden known to John Gerard [1545-1612] was that of William Coys of Stubbers, North Ockendon, who lived there from 1564-1627. Little was known about Coys until the letters of John Goodyear, the botanist, were published by Dr. Robert W T Gunther in 1922. Goodyear frequently acknowledges the assistance he had received from William Coys. Lobel the artist visited Coys's garden in 1604 to paint the first flowering of Yucca gloriosa in England in July of that year. It is also from this garden that the ivy-leaved toadflax, Cymbalaria muralis spread profusely throughout the country. Goodyear did not visit until 1617, but he returned to his Hampshire home with a list of Coys's plants that is the oldest manuscript of English garden plants correctly distinguished by botanical names. There were 324 plants that Coys had introduced into this country, which included rhubarb from Siberia and tomatoes and sweet and common potatoes from South America. Also from that continent he had the cherry Prunus virginiana and persimmon Diospyros virginiana. Little is known of his collectors, but William Boel did provide a fine collection of plants from Spain. Coys was much more than a plant collector, he was a propagator of new strains of primula and narcissus and was instrumental in changing the fermentation of beer by the introduction of hops. Stubbers was sold by his son Giles in 1647 for £2,000.

The Tudor gardens were very formal with flower beds of various geometric shapes planned within a main design enclosed by box and lavender hedges, trimmed into ornamental shapes. In large gardens there were terraces decorated with fountains, statues and vases, which had been inspired by the famous royal residence of Nonsuch. There are five examples of these gardens illustrated by private estate maps, Moulsham Hall in 1591 and Terling Place in 1597, Thorndon Hall in 1598, Ingatestone Hall in 1605 and Belhus in 1619.

Ingatestone Hall and Thorndon Hall give us the best example of what an Elizabethan garden was like because of the wealth of documentation and books on the subject. William Petre [1505?-72], Secretary of State, bought the manor of Gynge Abbess in Ingatestone, which had been part of the estate of Barking Abbey, for £849.12s.6d. after the dissolution and built Ingatestone Hall between 1540-5 on the site of Abbess Hall, not considered good enough for a man in his position.

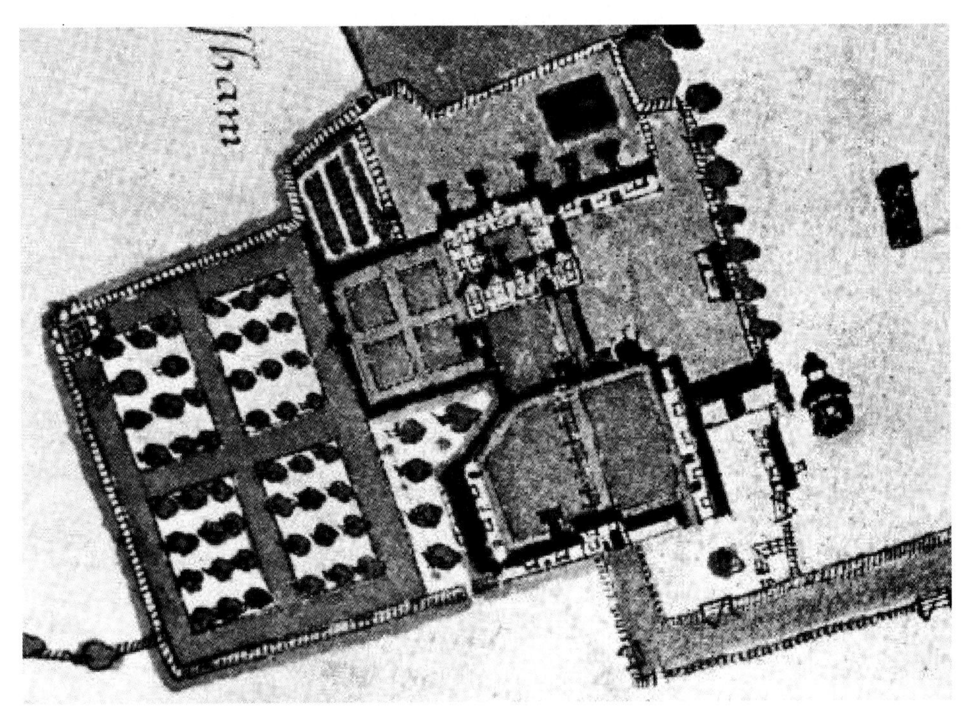

Moulsham Hall in 1591 (Reproduced courtesy of the Essex Record Office)

The private garden, nearly square, lay to the north-west of the house. It was divided into six rectangular beds and laid in the formal fashion of the day. The orchard surrounded the rest of the house except the west front. It was "well planted with young trees upon every bank and border of the best fruit that can be set in good order and proportion, one distant from another equally, and round the orchard to divers large walks, well kept and maintained." A bowling alley was mentioned in 1555 in the orchard, and a banqueting house lay in the south-west corner of the orchard. This was where the dessert course was taken in good weather. A cook's garden lay between the orchard and the stable block and a brick dovehouse provided food for winter, along with the well-stocked brewhouse pond. Petre also received a Crown licence to impark 300 acres as a deer park, but this was disparked by 1605 as Crondon Park provided all their venison supplies.

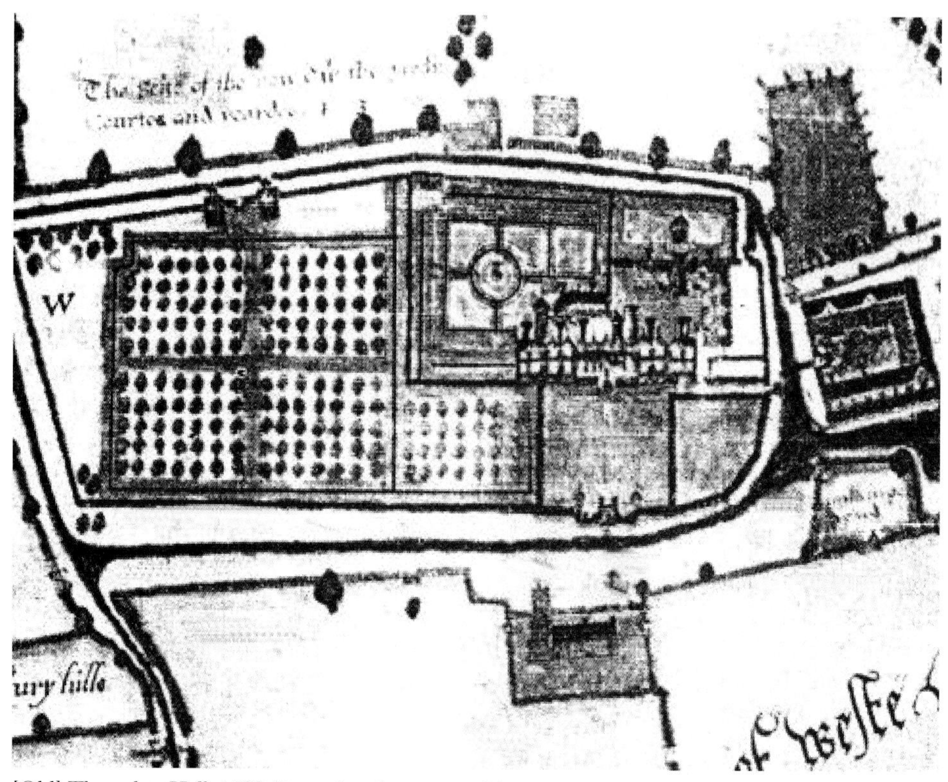

[Old] Thorndon Hall, 1598 (Reproduced courtesy of the Essex Record Office)

The only early account for vegetable seeds are amongst the household accounts of 1550 listing colwort seed 4d., parsley seed 4d., cersyll seed 2d., cucumber seed 2d., pompions [large onions] 8d., white beets 1d., and radish 2d. Also for this period the gardener's wages for the quarter year were 10s. 6d. with his wife earning a little for casual weeding.

John Petre, William's only son, inherited all the vast estates at the age of 21. It is thought that Sir William had nearly 20,000 acres in Essex and well over that amount in the west country. To this John added a further 2,700 acres in 1573 when he purchased Thorndon Hall in West Horndon; this was to remain the main family home for three centuries.

The house had been built around 1414/5 by Lewis John and enlarged 40 years later. Petre altered it considerably during the next 20 years. The gardens were also altered about 1589/90. Prior to this only one gardener is mentioned in the accounts; one Humphrey Hammond being paid 16s.8d. a quarter, but after this date Hammond is replaced by three gardeners, John Sperling, Adam Milad, who was highly paid at 30s. a quarter, and John Souton, obviously a boy from the wages. These appear to have begun the new layout as there is only one heading in the account books "charges for the orchard and garden" expenditure totalled £45.17s.6d.

Additional labourers were used for the removal of earth, a total of 459 days at 8 pence a day for filling carts with earth. This all resulted presumably in what was known as the Great Garden which lay to the north-west of the house being 130 yards square with geometric plots surrounded by brick walls. There was the main water supply to the house in the centre called the Great Vault and a white washed banqueting house in the north-west corner, with its hipped roof of blue slates. The kitchen garden lay to the east of this and the orchards to the west and south. The main orchard was 145 x 120 yards containing 145 fruit trees, with a smaller patch containing 28 trees. The old park of Thorndon lay to the north of the mansion, but Petre created a new park, probably only 50 acres. The old park was landscaped by 'Capability' Brown in the 1770s.

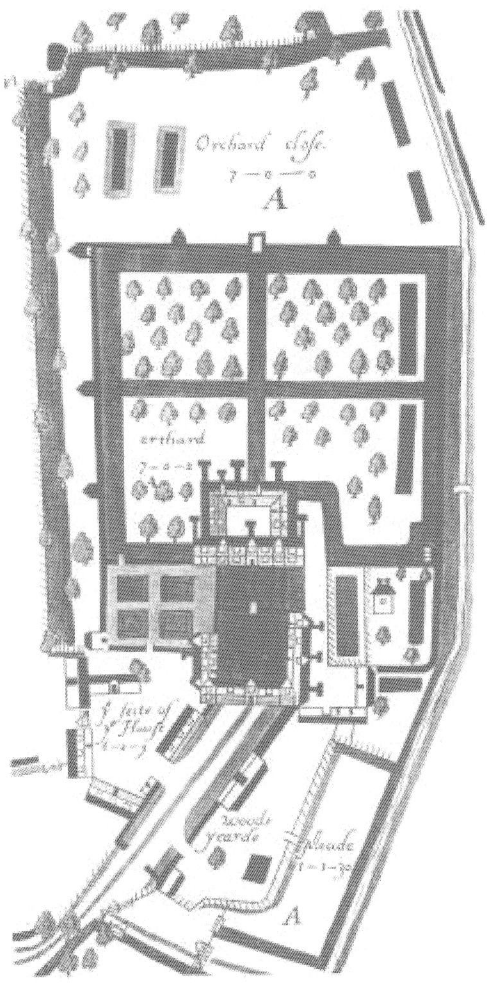

Both Ingatestone and Thorndon gardens can be seen with some clarity from the wonderful John Walker's estate maps. Thorndon's is dated 1598, Ingatestone is 1605 (illustrated on the left). The Walkers, father and son, both Johns, were remarkable cartographers; the accuracy of their buildings is incredible and of course, the gardens are nearly as good as an aerial photograph. They were local, their home being Kent's farm in West Hanningfield. These maps provide the only visual evidence of Elizabethan gardens in Essex. Together with Ingatestone Hall and Thorndon Hall, there are maps for Moulsham Hall in Chelmsford in 1591; this was built by Thomas Mildmay on what was a greenfield site formerly belonging to Westminster Abbey and was described as the "greatest esquire's building" in Essex in the second half of the 16th century. The map shows the house of courtyard type, in front are two more courts

The formal brick-walled garden lies to the south, with an orchard beyond, and the kitchen garden lies to the west. There is a brick dovecote near the farm buildings. Terling Place in 1597, New Peverells Hall in West Hanningfield in 1601 and Belchamp Hall in Belchamp Walter in 1605. Other early maps give a wealth of information on garden layout.

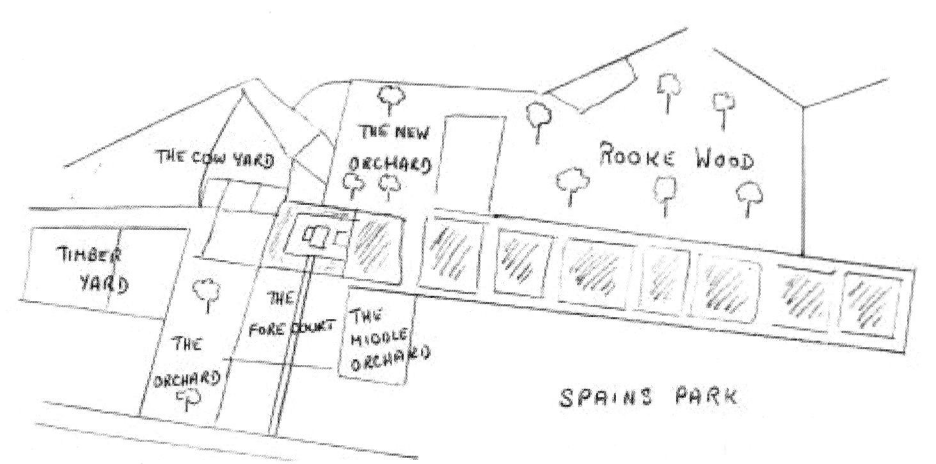

One of Spains Hall, Finchingfield, in 1618 drawn by Thomas Pope, shows a curious rectangular area containing 7 nearly equal square fish ponds, the old and new orchards and woodland; the parkland is covered in what look like delightfully drawn rabbits.

A Walker-style map shows the formal gardens and avenues at Hill Hall in Theydon Mount in 1657. These were probably the plantings from Sir Thomas Smyth's day. He acquired the property on the marriage to his second wife Philippa, daughter of Henry Wilford, a London merchant, and widow of Sir John Hampden of Essex; she bought with her the substantial estate of Theydon Mount, consisting of 1,000 acres of arable land, 500 acres of meadow and pasture and 400 acres of wood and heath, together with two large mansions, Hill Hall and Mount Hall, both of which he rebuilt. He was an avid gardener himself and was said to have personally planted and grafted the vines in his vineyard. A letter to his wife Philippa in March 1572, whilst he was in France mentions 'to have your vynes cut as nere the black stock, as convenyently may be, that is levyingut one cayne fro[m] it", and previously in January of the same year "that some dung be laid all along on the side of that long alley w[h]ich answereth to the wall that runith along dividying the P[ar]sones close and apece of Kichenfeld fro[m] my garden'. It seems he could never forget his garden even whilst away. The orchard is said to have been planted in 1568 or in late 1572 according to John Strype [1643-1737], his biographer, in 1698. The pear trees had been given by Lord Rich and the apple trees came from Saffron Walden. The elm avenue to the north of the house were "advancing their heads to a great Heighth' by this time, according to Strype and had been planted in double rows by Sir Thomas and were said to be 'fir for study and contemplation'; two of his fishponds remain in the garden as ornamental pools.

Despite parkland being disparked in the 17th century Sir Edward Barrett was granted a licence to make a park round Belhus in Aveley on 23 December, 1618, and to stock it with deer; by 1644 the deer numbered 300 and the park included oak, ash, elm and other timber. The garden at this period included a wilderness, a rock garden and a palisade garden that was presumably on the south side of the house where there was a walled forecourt.

When Lord Newburgh, as Sir Edward became, died, his widow married for a third time in 1650 and needed to raise money; much slaughtering of deer and trees ensued and an injunction had to be brought to stop her laying waste to the complete estate. Richard, Lord Newburgh's cousin, eventually acquired Belhus and took the name of Barrett as requested by Lord Newburgh.

John Tradescant [d.1637], one of the earliest plant collectors, was employed by George Villiers, Duke of Buckingham, at the New Hall estate in Boreham. He imported and planted many trees, including the wonderful lime tree avenue, planted in four rows in 1624. It was subsequently felled in 1798, but has been replanted as a single avenue. The walled garden, which has a remarkable double wall dividing the four acres was constructed at this time. It had an elaborate heating system concealed in the walls. The construction of the walls, tennis courts, bowling green and walks are mentioned in a letter to the Duke from his wife in 1623, who was the instigator of the landscape gardening at New Hall, together with her mother-in-law. John Evelyn, the diarist, visited the gardens in 1656.

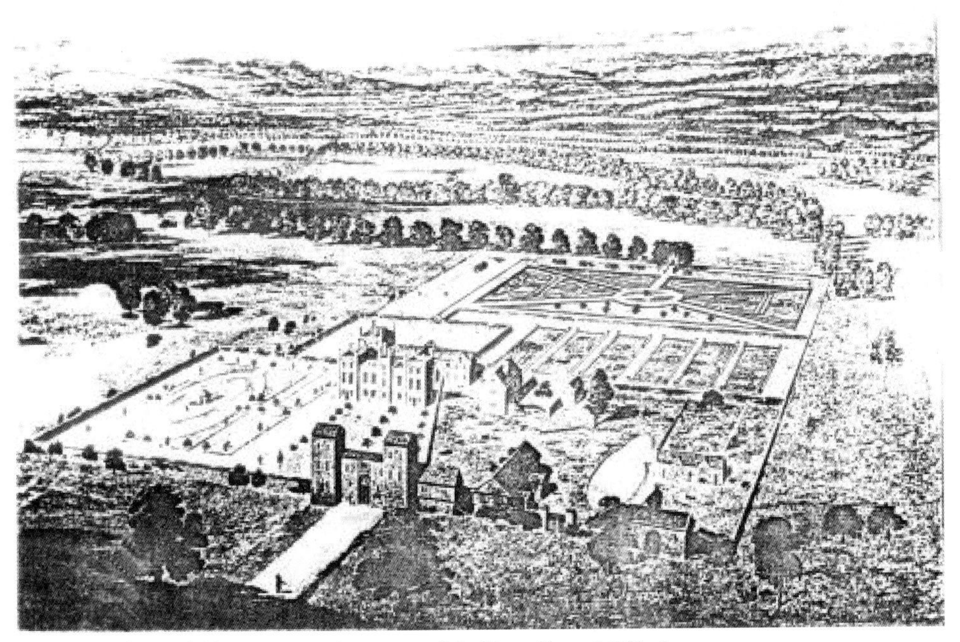

Belhus, Aveley, c.1710 (Reproduced courtesy of the Essex Record Office)

Chapter Two

The 18th Century
The Great Landscape Designers

The romantic inspirations of artists such as Claude Lorraine and Nicolas Poussin were the guiding light for the new era of 'landscape' gardening. The destruction of walls as boundaries and the inventions of the ha-ha has been considered by some as "probably the most important single innovation in the whole history of gardens". Instead of the garden harmonising with the house, the house now became part of the landscape. The constraining limitations of the formal parterres could no longer be accommodated. Joseph Addison writing in The Spectator in 1712 wrote, "Our British gardens, on the contrary, instead of humouring nature love to deviate from it as much as possible. Our trees rise in cones, globes and pyramids. We see the marks of the scissors upon every plant and bush. I do not know whether I am singular in my opinion, but, for my own part, I would rather look upon a tree in all its luxuriancy, than when it is thus cut and trimmed into a mathematical figure". Addison's condemnations had been placed specifically upon George London and Henry Wise [1653-1738] and their Brompton Nursery, started in 1689; their names being synonymous with formal gardening during the reigns of William and Mary and Queen Anne.

Sir Thomas Robinson, reporting in 1734 said that "there is a new taste in gardening just arisen which has been practised with so great success at the prince's garden in Town, that a general alteration of some of the most considerable gardens in the kingdom is begun." The Prince's garden was the fashionable garden laid out by William Kent [1684-1748] for the Prince of Wales at Carlton House, based on the pioneering work done by Alexander Pope at his garden in Twickenham. This was in complete contrast to the formal gardens of the previous century, providing winding paths through grassy glades, encircled by belts of trees and water always in the landscape.

The 18th century was the era of winding walks, serpentine lakes, cascades, grottos, romantic ruins and clumps and belts of tree plantations. It accelerated during the second half of the century with designers such as Brown landscaping hundreds of acres, the effect of which he only could envisage, and which we can now enjoy.

Our first landscape gardener to work in Essex was a former apprentice of London and Wise, but whose work was in considerable contrast; although more restrained than Woods, Brown and Repton that were to follow. Charles Bridgeman [d. 1738] appears in Essex during the early 1700s. His date and place of birth are not known, but he was working under London and Wise where he gained his practical gardening knowledge; he also trained as a surveyor. Bridgeman was a member of the St. Luke's Club where many of the leading artists of the day met, many of whom were also interested in garden design such as William Kent, Michael Rysbrack, the sculptor, Grinling Gibbons and James Gibbs. Through these people he gained employment on many landed estates.

He is known to have worked on three Essex gardens; the first was Langleys in Great Waltham. Samuel Tufnell acquired Langleys at Michaelmas in 1710 for £5,498 18s. 6d. From a 'particular' of about 1715 we know the park was only thirty four acres in extent with the house and its walled gardens, orchards, barns, and other outbuildings, together with a further eleven acres. The great horse chestnut here is reputedly the largest in the British Isles, and one of the first to be imported three hundred years ago. From his account books we know Tufnell was already working on the garden before Charles Bridgeman was involved. During 1713 he bought 19 apple trees and 1 pear tree for 15 shillings, a further 21 apple trees and 6 peach trees for £1 4s. 0d. and paid a Mr. Mason for further trees £6 3s. 0d. In 1712 his gardener's wages for the year were £8. Charles Bridgeman was employed in 1719 but we have no plans or information on what he was paid to do; only a receipt for £50 3s. 7d. together with a former amount of £106 3s. 7d. that was the full account for works and plants completed by him. Tufnell was still buying plants the following year; 35 standard cherries for £1 15s. and in 1726-7, 13,000 hop plants and 1,200 asparagus plants. The lead statuary, The Shepherd and Shepherdess, and the Eagles by the walled garden probably date from Bridgeman's time.

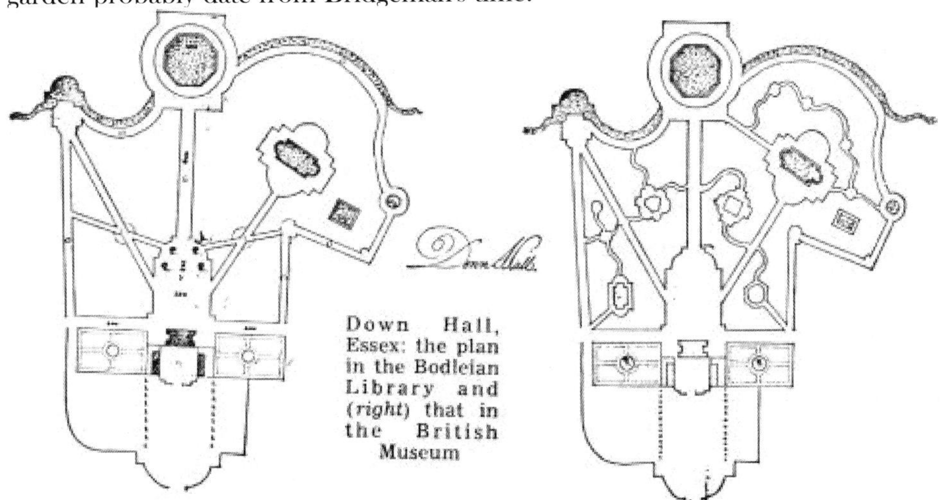

Down Hall, Essex: the plan in the Bodleian Library and (*right*) that in the British Museum

In 1720 Bridgeman was working at Down Hall, Hatfield Broad Oak. This was purchased by Edward Harley [1689-1741], later Earl of Oxford, in 1720 and given to his friend Matthew Prior for life. Bridgeman had probably obtained the commission from friends at the St. Luke's Club. Prior, a notable poet, commissioned James Gibbs to design a new house, and Bridgeman to replan the garden. Writing in 1720-1 to Harley, Prior says, "we have talked of nothing but canals, parades, and vistas from Wimpole to this place". In the next January the work had commenced "we have laid out squares, rounds and diagonals, and planted quincunxes at Down". Bridgeman was busy at Down Hall in the spring and summer of 1721, but all was abandoned when Prior died in the following September. Lord Harley did plant some trees in the grounds and removed others to reveal hidden vistas, and laid out a bowling green, but Bridgeman's great plans were not executed. These plans do survive, one in the Bodleian

Library, the other at the British Library, they differ in design, one being far simpler; one is thought to be Bridgeman's ideas, rather than Prior's. Both have the same rectangular kitchen gardens dither side; passing through the garden front to a terrace and lawn, there is a central avenue leading to an octagonal basin fed by a stream. Something of the outline of some of Bridgeman's work can still be seen in the woods north-west of the present house.

The only other commission Bridgeman is known to have had in Essex was Bower House in Havering-atte-Bower; again we have no plans or details. A painting of 1800 shows the house poised on a hillock within the park, a semi-circular woodland surrounds it studded with groups of oaks. The scene is very different now with town creeping around it.

Bridgeman succeeded Wise in the prestigious post of royal gardener at which he remained until his death in 1738. He was one of the first professionals to convert his ideas to paper and into reality, and the single figure to bridge the gap between the geometric formality of London and Wise's gardens to the classically inspired landscapes of William Kent.

Lancelot Brown [1715-1783] was born in Kirkharle, Northumberland, and was apprenticed to Sir William Loraine, a local landowner, on a small estate where he learnt the basic skills that were to serve him well throughout his life. By 1740 he was under-gardener at Stowe, Buckinghamshire for Lord Cobham. Cobham had had the best designers of the day working at Stowe - Vanbrugh, Bridgeman and Kent - who had all made Stowe a show piece of the time. Brown learnt much and probably carried out Kent's plans, but Kent worked on small areas, Brown wanted to work on a large scale. He would escort dignitaries around the gardens telling them of his own ideas and through this was already receiving commissions of his own. When Lord Cobham died in 1749, Brown felt qualified to engage in full time practice of designing gardens and moved to Hammersmith where he could meet landowners visiting the capital; he was also near to the market gardens and nurseries that surrounded London at this time. 'Capability' Brown as he became known, was based on his remark that all the land or gardens he surveyed had 'capabilities', is the most well-known of the landscape designers and much has been written about him, but he did not do a great deal of work in Essex.

His first design was at Belhus, Aveley, for the 17th Lord Dacre. He worked here between 1753-61; the grounds had been altered earlier in 1744, when the formal walled gardens, south of the house were removed, along with the gatehouse, which hindered the view of the park. Brown's earliest designs were for the shrubbery west of the house that utilised the existing Shaws or Small woods and about the same time he walled in the three acre kitchen garden. He then designed mounds to the north and north-east of the house, in order to break up the first appearance of the park, they were planted with exceptionally fine lime trees, one of which existed into this century. In 1761 the Long Pond was formed by excavating wet land and damming up the stream; it should have been ten acres in extent, but turned out little more than half that. He was paid a total of £668 14s. for the work. The house was demolished in 1957 and Belhus Park is now open to the public.

In 1758 Brown was paid £63 "for making a Pond at Shortgrove", Newport, for Percy Wyndham O'Brien, he was probably responsible for the boundary planting which survives, and the enlargement of the River Cam. A bridge was built over this between 1758-62, designed by Matthew Brettingham, the elder [1699-1769], who also added wings to the house and built a lodge. There must have been water gardens here before and canals, which are served with water thrown up from the river Cam by an engine, contrived by a Dr Desaguliers." Shortgrove Hall was burned down in 1966, the shell remains amongst the landscaped parkland. Brown's work on the Cam was reduced by the construction of the M11 motorway.

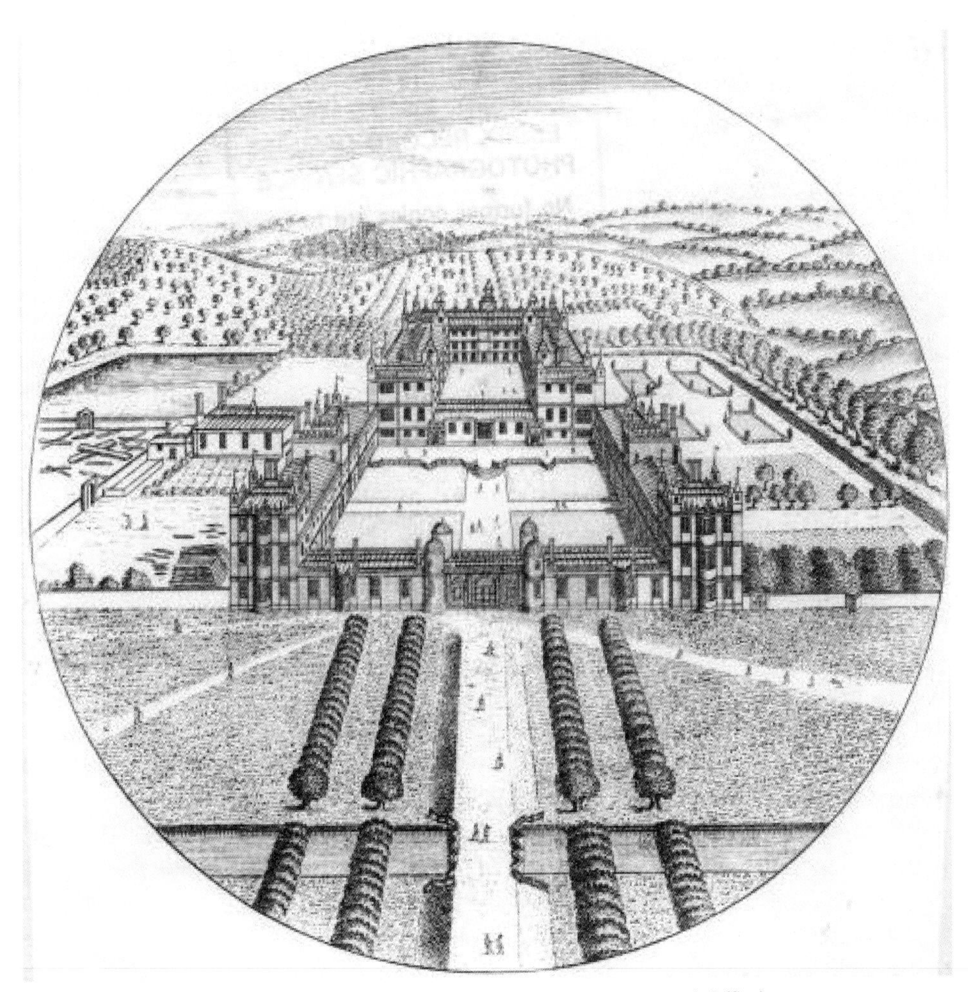

Audley End, as it was at its height (Reproduced courtesy of the Essex Record Office)

Between 1763 and 1766 Brown worked at Audley End, Saffron Walden. Early in the century, the house must have been in a bad state, according to Daniel Defoe, writing in 1726, "I saw the ruins of the once largest and most magnificent pile in all this part of England, Audley End." Brown listed seven main changes for the estate including Lady Griffin's garden, altering the course of the river, laying out the park and making a sunken fence or ha-ha, he even suggested the removal of two streets of houses that were too close to the house, and the diversion of roads running across the land; these were carried out by private Act of Parliament in 1764. The previous year a Grecian Temple was resited on a hill-top, west of the house, to commemorate the end of the Seven Years War: this was designed by Robert Adam, who was doing a considerable amount of work in the house. The amount of plants used in Brown's schemes were prodigious; in December 1766, 1,300 larches were planted; the following October a further 1,000 five feet high larches; in March 1768, 10,000 seedling scotch firs, and other trees including Weymouth lime, silver fir, Portuguese laurels, Caroline poplars and 'black' Canada larches and birches were planted. Silver firs, yews, and cedars were procured from Lord Montfort, and 3,000 Dutch alders came from Rotterdam.

Accounts for the same period tell us about the gardeners; Joseph Hicks supervised Brown's work. From 1 October to 31 December, 1766, there were nine gardeners, mostly digging, hoeing and sowing, but three were employed at this time earthing the oranges and myrtles and getting them in the house, and potting roses and carnations. In the first week they had been planting yews and laurels and potting auriculas. The gardeners during this period were John Bitton, John Boon, Robert Bunton, Will Duga, Samuel Powell, John Day, John Trowman and Robert Bradley; the latter two could have been apprentices, as their wages varied between 2s. 6d. and 4s. a week; the others could earn up to 7s. a week. The total wages bill for October 1766 was £11.16s.11d.

Brown's designs for Thorndon Hall, newly built by the 9th Lord Petre, utilised little of the magnificent grounds of the 8th Lord, and indeed often destroyed them, a plan of 1778 probably by J. Spyers, acting as Surveyor for Brown shows us what they looked like then. The lake south of the Hall was Brown's work, enlarged from an earlier pool, and the boundary plantations. He was here between 1766 and 1772. The parkland remains, some in the ownership of the Thorndon Park Golf Club, operating since 1919, and the rest acquired by the Essex County Council in 1939 for use as a country park.

Brown's other work was at Navestock between 1765 and 1782 for the 3rd Earl Waldegrave, a park and lake survives; Coopersale House in Epping in 1774 for John Archer, for which nothing is known; and in 1778 Brown was redesigning the park and gardens at Hallingbury Place for Jacob Houblon, a bill for £105 exists for a general plan and for lodges, but it is not known what was carried out.

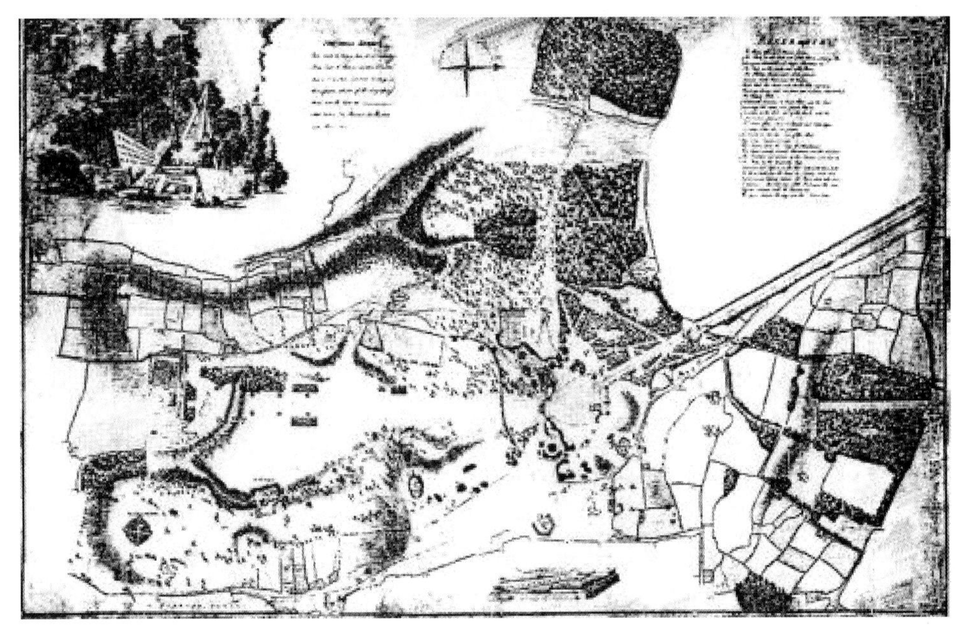

Thorndon Park in 1778 (Reproduced courtesy of the Essex Record Office)

Our third landscape designer of the 18th century was Richard Woods [1716-1793], who was probably born the same year as 'Capability' Brown, but it is not known where. Woods was not of the standing of Brown, although he instituted more work in Essex than Brown. He was working in Essex in 1763, but it was not until 1768 that he became an Essex resident as tenant at North Ockendon Hall, a property of Richard Benyon of Gidea Hall. North Ockendon Hall itself was described as a mansion standing in 250 acres with a 42 foot hot house, melon and cucumber frames and 136 foot of framing and lights for a peach wall. When his wife Hannah died, he left North Ockendon, married a Mary Gorst and had moved to a pair of cottages at Ingrave on the Petre estate, by November 1783. He became Lord Petre's surveyor for 10 years with a salary of £100 a year. Whilst here he probably designed the octagon lodge at Thorndon built c.1785.

As early as 1763 Woods was receiving money from Richard Hoare of Boreham House, but work did not really commence until 1771, so his earliest designs were in 1765; John Wright, M.P., of Hatfield Priory in Hatfield Peverel had a park of forty acres, Woods devised a simple design of two linked ponds which are still in existence, this plan was made three years before the old priory was demolished and a new one built, so the new house did not have a direct view of the water.

The same year Woods discussed plans with Isaac Martin Rebow who had just completed his new mansion at Wivenhoe Park in 1762. There is little record of these gardens before 1775, an odd bill for 1761 exists when 15s. was paid for 1,000 asparagus plants. In 1775, prior to Woods commencing his work, John Groves, gardener was paid 6 guineas every three months for looking after Madam Rebow's gardens and was occupied in stocking the garden with peaches, nectarines, cherries, grapes, plums and a mulberry tree. Richard Woods was delayed from starting at Wivenhoe while he was also working for Rebow's uncle and father-in-law, Thomas Martin at Alresford Hall, nearby. Here he built a delightful Chinese Temple on the lakeside and a fishing lodge designed for summer picnics. Woods spent 87 days at Wivenhoe between June 1776 and June 1779, for which he received £164.17s. The detailed estimate, probably dating from 1777, for the building works at Wivenhoe exists at the Record Office, the following is the estimated cost of the work involved:

Two large pieces of water and the heads and rustick arch be built at the upper end of the upper water £455

For making the strait canal with the border and walk next the wall and the hollow ditching the side of the hill hanging towards the said canal £100

Building bridge with bricks and with balustrade of oak £158 8s.

Making coach roads, levelling banks and filling holes £120

Lawn to be returfed and planting made it will be , £181

This meant that the water was being carried through the park at different levels; the first of the dams was constructed using the original bridge, the second, at the upper end of the water near the south-east corner of the kitchen garden, was also constructed in such a way as to require little brickwork, using a small arch to which pipes and valves were to be fitted to lower the level of water if required. It was to be four feet in depth, shallowing out at the sides. The second water was to cover existing hollow ground that was to be dug a further spit deep; the soil of which was to improve the lawn. The third head was to have been sited near the lower corner of the kitchen garden, but does not appear to have been constructed.

The workman's accounts for the period 1776-80 totalled £652.17s. This included casual labour and specialist workmen, but an average weekly pay roll came to about £2 10s. and the following are the list of gardeners at the time. Thomas Lupton being the foreman, and working directly with Woods.

6 - 11 March 1780

Thomas Lupton worked 5 days at 2s. 4d.	11s. 8d.
James Wright worked 6 days at 2s. 4d.	14s. 0d.
John Penn worked 4½ days at 1s. 6d.	6s. 9d.
Robert Jones worked 2 days at 1s. 6d.	3s. 0d.
Charles Cloar worked 5¼ days at 19. 6d	7s. 10½d.
William Ollis worked 4½ days at 1s. 6d.	6s. 9d.
Total	£2 10s. 0½

On 6 March 1780 Thomas Lupton reported "scattered trees are all planted betwixt the house and Wivenhoe Gate all tied to prevent the wind from loosening them". The seeds had all arrived but the frosts were too sharp to start planting. The list of trees planted on the east side of the park in 1780 consisted of :

200 Spruce firs @ 15s. per 100
100 Weymouth pine seedlings
50 Young cupress trees
400 Laurels mixed varieties
200 Larch trees of 2-3 ft. height
40 Newfoundland spruce firs
20 Red cedar

Two of Woods's lakes survive, and a third has been added by the University of Essex, who purchased the site in 1962. A house was built on the site of Woods's bridge. His grotto at the head of the lakes has been rebuilt in red brick since the University ownership, but the ice house survives close by. John Constable painted the house and landscape in 1816.

Woods was paid £250 in 1767 by Lord Waltham, and a further £455 in 1775-6 for work at New Hall; these sums of money are the only possible proof that it was Woods who executed the work which Muilman in 1768 describes as "laying out the gardens and park with such taste as to render the situation delightful. He is making a noble sheet of water in the new gardens behind the house, and erected near it an exceeding good green house.' The Chapman and André map of 1777 includes "the noble sheet of water' which is similar to Woods's other work. The greenhouse, also similar to those that Woods designed elsewhere, can be seen on a painting by James Luttrell of 1778.

In 1768/9 Woods was employed by John Wallenger, in conjunction with Paine in the building of Hare Hall, Romford, but there are no surviving plans. W Angus, writing in his Seats of the Nobility, states that the gardens and pleasure grounds were laid out by Mr. Wood of Essex, and a plan in a sale catalogue of 1895 does show a typical Woods design. There is a wonderful description of the grounds in Neale's, Views of Seats " The grounds ... of triangular form, are entered by a neat lodge ... a beautiful canal meanders and passes the East End of the House, on the opposite side of which is a Terrace, called the Elysian Walk; this was raised with the earth taken up to form the canal: from this is a communication at the back of the Elms to a Serpentine Walk, nearly a mile in length, the sides of which are planted with curious shrubs and evergreens, and ordered by a gay profusion of Flowers; this Terrace extends to the Lodge and, occasionally a break in the foliage admits a view of the adjacent Country. Amid the verdant scene the canal has the appearance of a winding river: a Stone Bridge is seen at one of its terminations, the other extremity is lost in a cluster of Weeping willows... " Nothing remains of the landscape except the flint-faced brick bridge.

As will have been seen in the previous account, Brown worked at Belhus from 1753-63, but it is believed that the final form of the long pond was the work of Richard Woods, who received £275 from Lord Dacre between 1770-71. The bridge that crossed the pond near its tail was built in 1772 at a cost of £42 by one Richardson, who may have been under Woods.

This was a busy period for Woods in Essex, he was back at Boreham House, having had earlier dealings there. He converted an existing stream at the back of the house into a lake; 261 barrow loads of clay were used us a retaining wall for the river. Woods's expenditure during 1771-2 was £653.7s.22d. with garden labourers paid at a daily rate of 1s.4d. - 1s.8d. or for piece work. Edward Pugh, the foreman, was paid 3s. 6d. a day from May 1771 to July 1772 working 6 days a week. Boreham House remains much the same as in Woods's day, the double avenue of elms planted by the Tyrell family, either side of the lake, in front of the house, have been replanted in this century with sweet chestnut, but the water at the back of the house remains.

While Pugh superintended work at Boreham House, Woods was working at Great Myles, in Kelvedon Hatch, for John Luther. In December 1771 he was paid for "making the new river and forming the ground on both sides of the same", this involved damming a tributary of the River Roding to form a long expanse of water in front of the house; "for building the new bridge over the said river", which was a graceful brick bridge that still exists, and "for a collection of plants to furnish the ground about the water', the total cost being £903.14s. An inventory of 1787 mentions the summer house, which could have been designed by Woods also.

Richard Benyon [d. 1796] of Gidea Hall, Woods's landlord at the time, probably had Woods draw the designs for the enlarging of his park c.1776. He made it less formal and introduced a lake in the valley west of the house; the greater width of water at the main road made a new bridge necessary; this was designed by James Wyatt with a three arched span, he also designed the Grecian temple.

An interesting inventory and gardener's agreement survives for Gidea Hall in 1793 between Richard Benyon and Solomon Stubbing; he had to provide 30 loads of dung to be spread a year, to scour ditches and watercourses, maintain paths, lawns, clip hedges, prune trees, shrubs and vines, maintain all hothouses, frames and tools, and he was allowed to pasture one horse free! An inventory of goods for which Solomon Stubbing would have been responsible, and a valuation of the crops in the ground also survives for the same date is on the following page.

The property was sold after Richard Benyon's death and the Sale Catalogue of 1797 gives a description of the garden at that time: the garden was of 32 acres in extent, mostly walled and planted with choicest fruit trees, a walled in melon ground, a small hothouse, the pleasure grounds and lawns beautifully laid out and intersected with walkways ornamented with plantations and groves of lofty timber. There were several large canals well stocked with fish, a cold bath well supplied from a fine spring and a large greenhouse with a stewards' office.

Gidea Hall was demolished in 1930, the Gidea Park Garden Suburb having been built in the grounds in 1910/11. The lake, however, known as Black's Canal, the name synonymous with Alexander Black whose name has also been attributed to the bridge, is now included in Raphael Park, the fish ponds survive further east. Near them in Heath Drive are sections of garden walling from Gidea Hall, probably of the early 18th century.

Work had not been forthcoming and Woods was getting into financial difficulty, but in November 1780 he received £35 from Sir John Griffin Griffin for "surveying and drawing the intended cascade, etc." for an Elysian garden at Audley End. This was created in a damp meadow next to the kitchen garden north west of the house. Woods's design shows a cascade taking water from the mill stream, which had belonged to the abbey, to the long pond. A description of this was given in a contemporary newspaper: "The water calls itself two miles long - 60 feet wide, and 4 to 12 feet deep - it has a 6 feet fall, which well flung about in a cascade, with flowers scenting all round it - the bridge and Ionic, Colonnade and church to see - the music in the evening to hear - make up the charm of the place; and so, falling when we should feel, they call it Elysium." The excessive dampness led to the failure of the Elysian garden, but it still retained its charm.

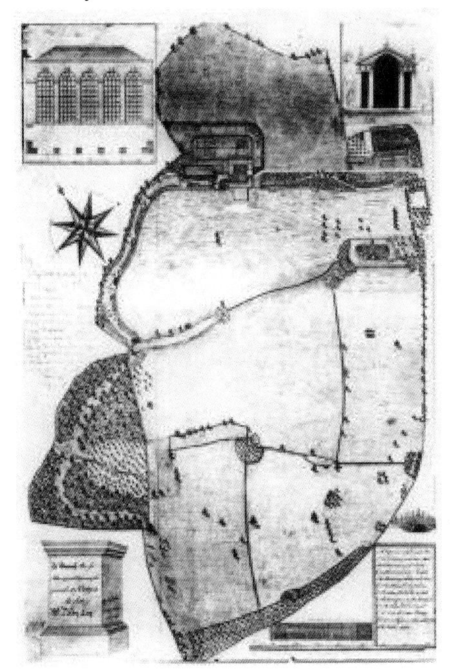

In 1781 Woods was working for Thomas King at Rectory Farm in Bardfield Saling, this was probably quite small scale, and I have found no details of this. His next work in Essex was Copford Hall where he was employed by John Haynes Harrison from 1784 Woods's plan for the improvement of Brizes, 1788 to1792. It had contained a series of rectangular ponds combined with a small formal garden surrounded by hedged fields. Woods improvements altered the water feature; the north and north-west ponds were linked together, where they met he designed a grotesque arch cascade. His plans show the layout of the buildings, the gardens, home farm and herbery, park, plantations with varieties of trees, ornamental waters, "Bowling Green Saloon" and 'Rosery Saloon" with inset drawings of the "Grotesque Arch and Cascade" and "Little Bridge and Cascade" that consisted of 133 acres in total

Woods's last known commission was in 1788 at Brizes in Kelvedon Hatch, for William Dolby. The plan alone survives, the work appears to have been carried out, as Woods's ideas are shown on the first edition 6 inch Ordnance Survey of 1876. The basic design is still visible, with the inner and outer walls of the kitchen garden still standing with rounded corners as found elsewhere in Woods's work, and there were remains of "such fences with quick hedges" as marked on his plan. It also included "an alcove seat or temple", "the truss Palladian bridge" and plantations of oak, chestnut, pine and elms and other features covering 74 acres.

At the time of Woods's death in 1793 he was working on a piece of land in Stanway adjoining the Copford Hall estate, both owned by John Haynes Harrison. After his death, his widow Mary tried to get the £50 18s. 6d. owed to him by Mr. Harrison, the account was for 'a plan and elevation for the Gothic Lodge, for the bailiff" and a survey of farms in Stanway "to which is added a plan for the improvement and ornamenting the same', but Harrison had abandoned the improvements and only paid £21 for the plan itself. A letter from William Bullock, solicitor, of 10 July, 1794, requested further payment of £29 17s. 6d. that was still outstanding to Richard Woods.

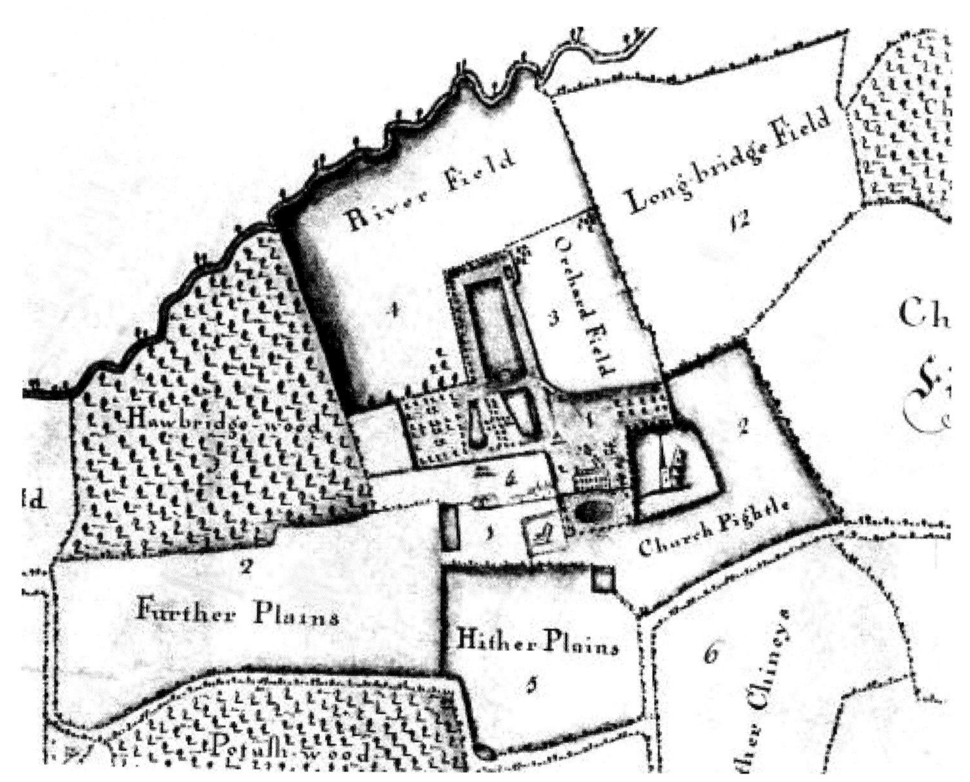

Copford Hall. Survey of 1766 by Skinner – before Woods's improvements
(Reproduced by courtesy of the Essex Record Office)

The last of the great 18th-century landscape designers was Humphry Repton [d. 1818]. He was born at Bury St. Edmunds, Suffolk in 1752, and married early with an unsuccessful early life, but had studied botany for five years assisted by James Edward Smith [1759-1828], a noted botanist of the day.

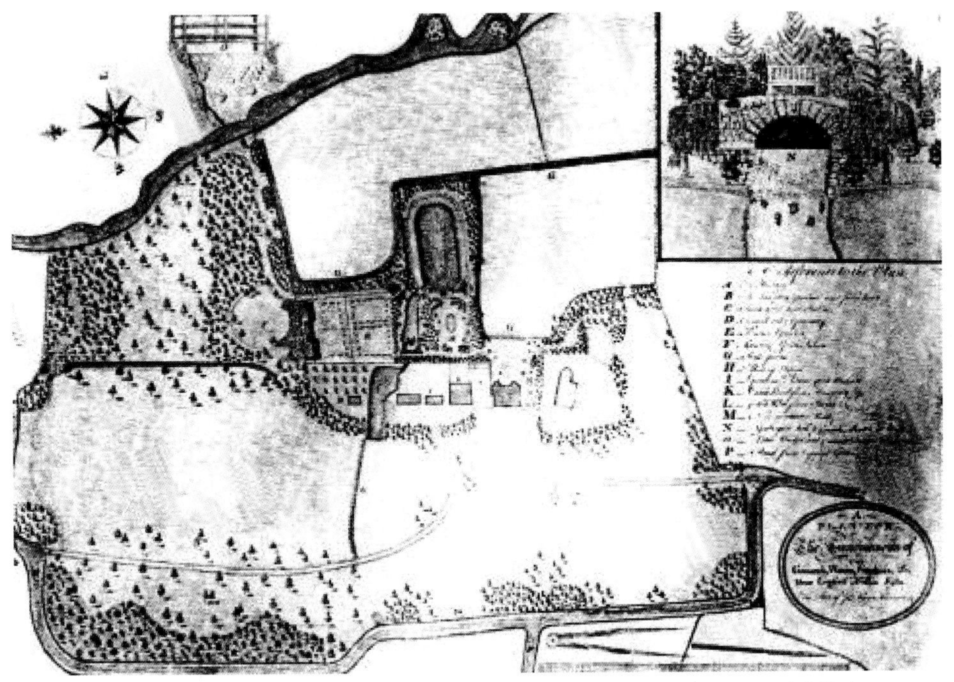

Richard Woods's plan of 1784 (Reproduced by courtesy of the Essex Record Office)

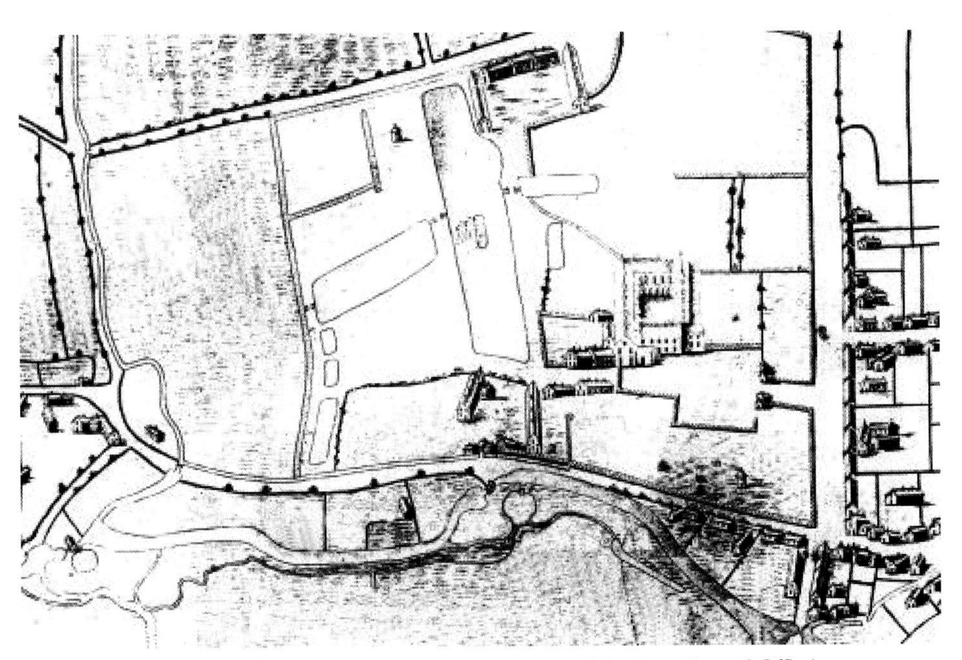

The Audley End Abbey before 1600 (Reproduced by courtesy of the Essex Record Office)

Humphry Repton's cottage at Hare Street, Romford – before and after.
(Reproduced by courtesy of the Essex Record Office)

He had moved to Hare Street, Romford, but still had no career; many business ventures that he tried having failed. In 1788, being short of money, he decided to follow in the footsteps of Brown who had died five years previously. He was well suited for the task, having an excellent knowledge of botany and being a first class draughtsman. Like Brown, Repton too found it necessary to 'improve' the buildings to fit in with the 'improved' landscape. This aspect of his work was heightened in 1795 by his partnership with John Nash, who provided the architectural impetus that Repton lacked.

After following Brown's ideas, he soon created his own style. Writing in 1806, he said that " perfection of landscape gardening consists in the four following requisites: First, it must display the natural beauties and hide the natural defects of every situation. Secondly, it should give the appearance of extent and freedom, by carefully disguising or hiding the boundary. Thirdly, it must studiously conceal every interference of art, however expensive, by nature only. And fourthly, all objects of mere convenience or comfort, if incapable of being made ornamental or of becoming proper parts of the general scenery, must be removed or concealed. This latter article, I confess, has occasionally misted modern improvers into the absurdity of not only banishing the appearance, but the reality of all comfort and convenience to a distance; frequently exemplified in a bad choice of a spot for the kitchen garden."

Repton re-introduced the terrace, not only enriching the foreground but as a useful base for the house to stand upon. The 'avenue' was no longer frowned upon and he also brought back flower-beds and small specialized flower gardens. All his designs were placed in individual 'Red Books', so named because of the colour of the binding. They included a survey of the property and an explanation of the changes required. A picture of the area was always included with another picture super-imposed by means of a flap, so the before and after picture could be viewed simultaneously. Repton merely arranged for the designs, he never oversaw the work, which was carried out by the clients themselves. The existence of these books of course, does not mean that Repton's work was ever carried out to his instructions or ever done at all.

More Essex gardens had Repton's touch, than the three previous designers, possibly because he already lived in Essex. His first Essex work was in 1789 for Montague Burgoyne at Marks Hall, Harlow, but there are no details as to what he advised: the area has been built over by Harlow New Town.

Also in 1789 Repton visited Rivenhall Place, the home of Charles Callis Western, [1767-1844] M.P. There is no surviving 'Red Book', but Repton's account book does survive that tells us his first visit to Rivenhall was on 31 August, again in September and November and two further visits in May and September of the following year. His comments were not favourable on Rivenhall. 'The present character of Rivenhall Place is evidently gloomy and sequestered, with the appearance of being low and damp. The first object is to remove the stables, and all the trees and buses in the low meadow, which may then with ease be converted into a pleasing piece of water, in the front of the house.

Rivenhall Place after Repton's work (Reproduced by courtesy of the Essex Record Office)

In its present state, two tall elm trees are the first objects that attract our notice, from the tops of those trees the eyes measure down to the house that is indistinctly seen amidst the confusion of bushes and buildings with which it is encumbered; thus we conclude that the house stands low. But get rid of this confusion and let the water be the leading object and the eye will naturally measure upwards to the house, it no longer appears in a low situation.' He took the drive curving round to the south, then across the newly formed lake and up towards the house. The bridge was designed by William Wilkins [1778-1839] from Norwich for three guineas. Wilkins probably assisted him with designs for the house. Western soon tired of Rivenhall Place and put his efforts into nearby Felix Hall in Kelvedon, where again Repton was supposed to have been consulted, but there is no information regarding this. There are two maps of Rivenhall Place that show the garden layout, the first surveyed in 1716 by Benjamin Fellowes of Maldon, shows a large fish pond, orchard, kitchen garden, and two squares of formal garden with radiating avenues of trees leading to roundels, presumably of trees. The later, of c.1825, shows the enlarged stretch of water, a kitchen garden, and parkland, the earlier features having disappeared. Now the parkland has disappeared under the plough.

The next year, 1790, there were plans for the following Essex gardens: Highams, Stansted Hall and Warley Lodge. At Stansted Hall, few changes were made, the lake, although in the wrong place, had to remain as making a new one would have taken land too valuable to be lost under water, and would not be seen from the house. Repton usually did things in a very practised way, usually removing hedges and planting trees and changing roads to give a different view of the house.

The house at Woodford, owned by Richard Puller, and Warley Lodge, for Sir George Allanson-Winn, there is no useful information for. The 'Red Book' does survive for Highams at the Vestry House Museum. It was built in 1768 for Anthony Bacon, but changed hands frequently. In 1785-90 William Hornby removed the pediment to add a balustraded third floor. It was this floor that Repton commented on as being 'extravagantly lofty' when he was commissioned to work on Highams for John Harman in 1793-4. He suggested ways of getting rid of this height, but the only garden work was the creation of a lake that still survives in what is now Highams Park, a public open space.

In 1791 Repton was called in to advise James Hatch on his new possession of Claybury Hall, Woodford. He had taken possession in 1788 of a much neglected site and rebuilt the house, but Repton admitted that 2 little remains to be done in comparison with what has already been executed'. The house was in an enviable position with magnificent views over several counties and Repton, writing in his book, says that "when nature has been so bountiful of charms as in the situation of Claybury, Art can seldom greatly interfere without violating the genius of the place ... and ... where Art cannot increase the natural charms, she is only to give comfort and convenience without disturbing what she cannot improve.' The only major alteration Repton made was the re-siting of the drive, and the main entrance to the north of the house, as he thought it impossible for a lady to get into a coach if the wind was too strong! He recommended the keeping of a small flock of sheep to keep the turf trimmed and a rustic cottage to be built for security. Samuel Prout writing in his notebook in July 1804, gives a lovely insight into Claybury.

Claybury Hall (Reproduced by courtesy of the Essex Record Office)

"On the south side [of the house] Mr. Hatch has built a large conservatory in which are many rare and valuable plants. The grounds are well wooded, and rise behind the house ... Near the house cloathed in wood is a small but curious grotto created by Hatch. The outside is formed by trunks of trees. The inside with shells, spars and minerals, on the windows is represented Faith, Hope and Charity, on the door the arms of the family painted by Mrs. Abdey, on the floor five feet in diameter is laid with horses' teeth." Claybury is now a hospital, and Repton would not be enraptured at the view!

Hill Hall, Theydon Mount, one of the vistas from the Red Book

Also in 1791 Repton was called in by Sir William Smyth to advise on the grounds of Hill Hall, Theydon Mount. He suggested many alterations to boundaries, including moving the public road east of the church, which then incorporated the church in the park. The drive to the house was impeded by the kitchen garden, which he re-sited. The courtyards were not suitable to turn carriages in, so he advised that the principal entrance to the house be removed to the south side. The entrance to the park was through a plantation that surrounded the pond. Sheltered walks and garden buildings were created to give comfort during the winter months.

Repton was at Stubbers, North Ockendon in 1796, for William Russell. Unfortunately he was instrumental in destroying William Coys garden. He did keep the lime tree walk and a wall on the west side of Coys garden, but the other walls were destroyed and a ha-ha put in to give a 'pastoral view'. He built a crinkle-crankle wall and a new vegetable garden concealed in a meadow beyond a large pool. He suggested that the neighbouring road should be diverted further west; this was not carried out until 1814. The 'Red Book' does exist, but is damaged. The house was demolished in 1960 and the land is under the control of the Essex Federation of Boys' Clubs, but a major restoration programme is going on under the Friends of Stubbers Walled Garden.

Between 1797-1803 Repton was advising on Hylands House, near Chelmsford. Cornelius Hendrickson Kortright had bought the estate in 1797 for £14,500 from the Comyns family, who had owned the house since Sir John Comyns built it in 1728-30. It originally had an old formal geometric garden laid out adjacent to the east wing. To the north was a pleasure garden and a small greenhouse that supplied the house with fruit and vegetables. Kortright wanted grander things and Repton was employed to redesign the house and grounds. He surrounded the park with belts of trees, added an artificial canal to the north of the estate and built a ha-ha around the house. He added drives around the house and built a kitchen garden. He extended the park to the River Wid, and built a new lodge at the Widford entrance. He constructed a walled garden containing a greenhouse to the north of the house and excavated a deep lake in the pleasure garden. An ice-house was also built near the lake.

Woodford Hall was his next assignment in 1801, for John Maitland. The house was surrounded on three sides by either roads or buildings; the church was in one direction and the farm in another. Repton suggested removing walls and roads surrounding the house, and building the front of the house with a columned entrance to remove the many steps to the door. To take full advantage of the vista of lawn and woodland, he suggested the removal of the kitchen garden to the right of the property and putting the poultry houses in the woodland. A flower garden with irregular shaped pool was to be put near the church yard and more irregular shaped flower beds could be provided in this area, or an American garden could be created with trees and shrubs. He suggested the removal of some of the trees in the avenue, which he considered too straight.

About 1803 Repton was consulted by Charles Smith, M.P., of Suttons, South Shoebury and by Samuel Jolliffe Tufnell of Langleys, Great Waltham, but I have found nothing for these two houses. Repton was at Warley Place in 1806, again little is known of what he did, and the wonderful garden of Ellen Willmott was still nearly a century away. The south lodge was certainly attributed to Repton.

Repton was at Spains Hall, Finchingfield in 1807. This was part of the remodelling plans of Thomas Ruggles [1737?-1813], who had acquired the property in 1784. A barrister by profession, his impetus in life was the agricultural labouring poor. During the agricultural depression, which inflated wheat prices, Ruggles suggested the growing of potatoes for labourers and animals. He was fervently interested in horticulture and studied Linnaeus, Pennat and John Ray. Arthur Young [1741-1820], F.R.S., was a personal friend and with whom he had been at school in Lavenham, Suffolk. Edith Freeman's book about the family has a lovely little story about one of Young's visits: 'Young was delighted to find that Ruggles had instituted a fish book and entered details of stocking and drawing fish from the various ponds over the years 1784-1791. In 1791 there was no record, the perch had eaten all the carp! Young scolded him for his neglect and left him to renew and fill the three empty ones and to be more attentive in stocking and emptying them. His determination was short lived if we are to believe his accounts with his fishmonger."

Spain's Hall, Finchingfield

Repton made a sketch modifying the eight ponds; the second and third were put into an irregular shaped lake, the sixth was to be extended to the west. The plantations to the left and right of the lake are supposed to be from his influence. Existing iron rose-hoops are thought to be from Repton's day. When Thomas Ruggles died, in his will, a codicil of which was written in 1811, he bequeathed £20 to his gardener Robert Finch. Thomas's son John was devoted to farming and thought highly of the estate, planting 6,000 trees, either in plantations or as specimens. His father had previously planted many trees in the hedgerows. In 1824 John Adey Repton, Humphry's son, painted two watercolours for his proposals to re-model the house in 'Tudor' style, but an anonymous artist shows us a 'Reptonesque' view of the garden at this period; this could be one of the watercolours. This 'Tudor' style was used for the three new entrance lodges, which John had built; he also restored and enlarged the old Tudor garden walls that form a backdrop for the herbaceous borders. He also built the banqueting or prayer house in the 1830s.

Moor Hall in Harlow was his assignment in 1808 to coincide with the rebuilding of the house between 1805-10. In his report of 11 May 1808 he writes: 'after so much has been done to improve this place, little remains for me to suggest'. He did re-shape a chain of natural lakes, but his greatest improvement was the re-siting of the road. He suggested removing the original and replacing it with a straight road that took the public away from the house, and with the new ground planted with trees. It gave a good entrance; as this would now be further from the house, a lodge was to be built here also, and the stables also were to be moved, either hidden by plantations, or placed to advantage with an ornamental façade. The valley called the Moor had been used with little interest; he suggested calling this 'The Thornery', and to have a thatched covered seat near the Chalybeate Spring where one could sit "amidst the murmur of trickling rills - and the song of the Nightingales that peculiarly abound in this part of the premises".

Moor Hall, 1833

The road diversion was given consent on 18 September 1810, but John Perry, the owner died that same year and the valuation of his estate at December 1810 for £21,120, gives a description of the garden: 'The gardens enclosed with lofty substantial brick walling, and abundantly planted and stocked with the choicest fruit. The pleasure grounds enclosed and planted with stately timber, exoticas and ornamental shrubs and situate in very desirable situation' extended to about ten acres.

The army occupied the house during the Second World War and left to decay; it was burned by vandals and finally demolished c.1960. In 1978 part of the stable block and one of the lodges survived and some of the 19th-century landscape could still be seen, as it was left as green belt area for the new town of Harlow.

In 1811 the philanthropist, William Cotton [1786-1866] of Wallwood, Leytonstone, employed Repton, but we know not for what. The house and land has been built over. The same year he was supposed to have submitted plans for Wanstead House, but with the problems that were beginning there at that period as I have reported in another chapter, it is doubtful whether any work was carried out. Dagnams at Romford Common was his last Essex assignment, where he improved a lake for Sir Thomas Neave. A letter of 31 March 1816 mentions three visits by Repton, for which he was paid twenty guineas.

Chapter Three

The 18th Century
Garden Transformations

The 18th century was the most prodigious period of gardening in general. Many estates were refurbishing or rebuilding their properties and gardens alike. Apart from work carried out by the four previous garden designers, there were many others and owners themselves creating their own piece of 'paradise'.

There are account books, engravings, maps and suchlike that give an insight into garden changes of the landed gentry during this period. One of the greatest houses of this time was Wanstead House.

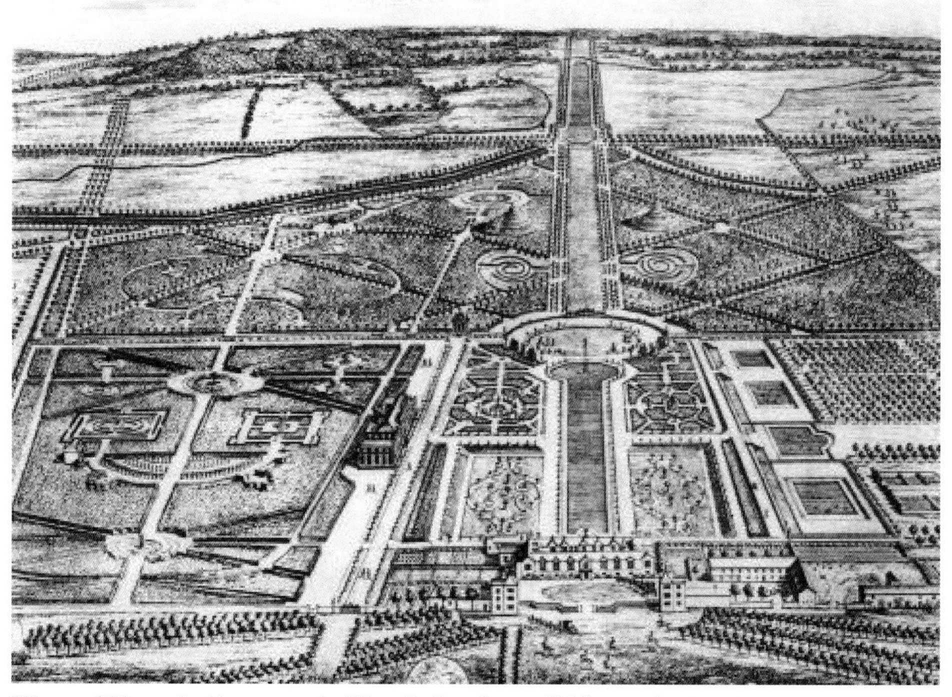

Wanstead House, looking east to the River Roding, from a 1715 engraving (Essex Record Office)

Josiah Child, who had amassed his fortune whilst being the director of the East India Company, bought the Wanstead estate c.1673-4 and proceeded to spend on his acquisition, especially the gardens. The diarist John Evelyn visited in 1683 and commented on the new fishponds, many miles in circumference and the prodigious cost of the Walnut plantations. Sir Richard Child succeeded to the estate in 1706 and reputedly employed George London to further design the garden. An engraving of 1715 shows the magnificent layout of the gardens, and the old house, prior to its demolition.

A canal runs eastward from the house with a bowling green at the far end, flanking which was a formal parterre. To the south of the house lay the kitchen gardens and opposite them the greenhouse and banqueting house.

The new house was designed by Colin Campbell and is thought to be the first Palladian house in England. By 1722 the house, without the wings, was standing amongst Josiah's garden. It was said to have cost £360,000 and the garden the same again. A French landscape gardener, J. Rocque, designed the new gardens for Wanstead in 1735. The plan removed the formal parterre and substituted a terrace and vast lawn. The bowling green, banqueting house and palizado had been swept away. All the formality had been removed and replaced by serpentine walks that opened unexpectedly into glades and amphitheatres, only the two mounds remained of the earlier garden. It covered 100 acres and was said to be one and a quarter miles long, three-quarters of a mile westward of the house and a half mile east to the river Roding. Together with the park it covered 300 acres. To the south, large new ornamental waters were created, one containing an island, supposedly representing the map of England, Scotland and Wales, while to the north-east a labyrinth of canals had been cut from the river. The lake to the west of the house was enlarged to form an octagon called the Basin. The plan also shows details of the little amphitheatre, the garden house, the mount, the stove house, the great stove house, the fortifications and the mount in the great lake in miniature sketches.

The second Earl Tylney, Richard having been created the first, built the grotto c.1762 at a cost of £2,000, but a further £40,000 was reputedly spent on its embellishment with shells, pebbles and crystals. He was probably responsible for the building of the temple on the eastern side of the park. The orangery that is shown on the 1715 engraving was demolished in 1799.

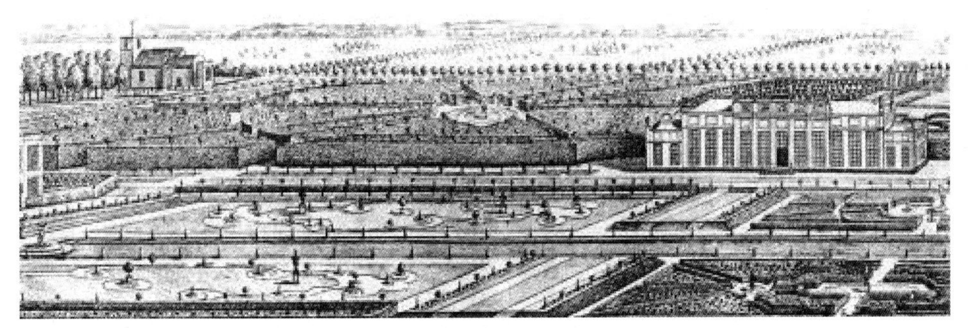

The Orangery (Reproduced by courtesy of the Essex Record Office)

Daniel Defoe in his Tours Through the Eastern Counties writes highly of Wanstead: "Sir Richard Child ... laid the most delicious, as well as most spacious pieces of ground for garden that is to be seen in all this part of England. The greenhouse [152 feet long] is an excellent building fit to entertain a prince; it is furnished with stoves and artificial places for heat from an apartment in which is a bagnio and other conveniences, which render it both useful and pleasant. And these gardens have been so the just admiration of the world, that it has been the general diversion of the citizens to go out to see them, till the crowds grew too great, and his lordship was obliged to restrain his servants from showing them, except on one or two days in a week only.'

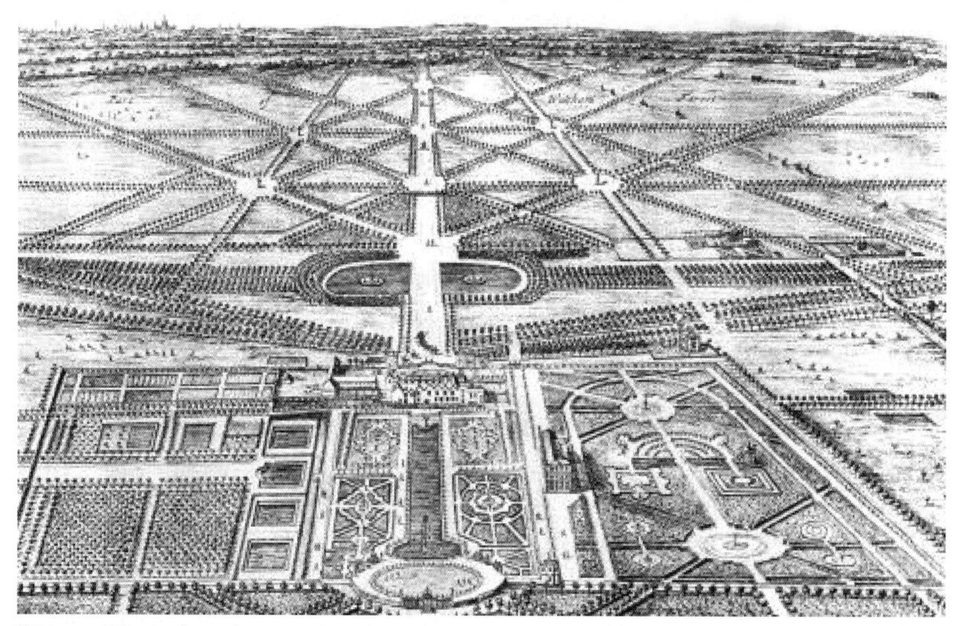

Wanstead House from the west, 1715 (Reproduced by courtesy of the Essex Record Office)

Wanstead met its demise in the early 19th century; Catherine Tylney Long, several generations removed from the 1st Earl Tylney, Richard Child, was considered at the time of her marriage to be the most wealthy heiress in England other than Royalty, but unfortunately she married the wrong man in William Pole Tylney Long Wellesley; a nephew of the Duke of Wellington; he had to take the names of Tylney Long upon marriage. Within 10 years he had squandered her fortune and was in severe debt; he fled with his family to the continent. An auction was held in June 1822 of the furniture and art treasures; the sale lasted 32 days but did not raise the sum needed. The house was put up for sale, but no buyer was found; it was sold for demolition materials only, the following year, realising just £10,000.

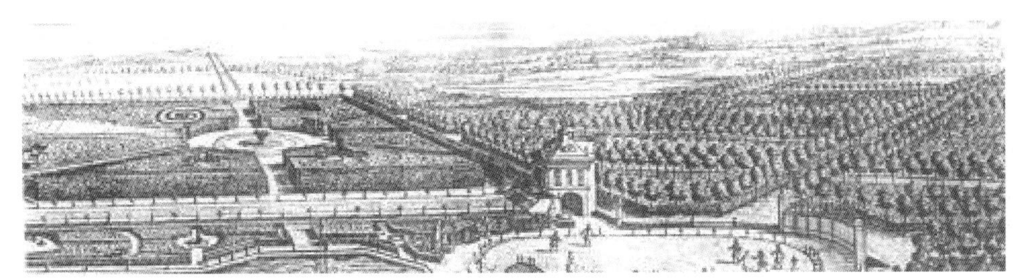

Another view, showing the bowling green and the garden house (Reproduced by courtesy of Essex Record Office)

Despite now being in the London Borough of Redbridge, some of the landscape does remain. The house used to stand where the Wanstead Golf course now is, the 18th century stable block being used as the club house. The Corporation of London purchased 184 acres on 1 August 1882 as a public park, where the water features such as The Green Man pond to the west, the Basin, and the chain of artificial waters, Lincoln Island pond, the Straight and the Serpentine pond which includes the Perch Pond and the Boating lake and Shoulder of Mutton pond remain in some form; the site of the Great Lake where stood the Lake House, the one time home of the poet Tom Hood, has been filled in and built over, as has much of the area.

Wanstead House, 1783

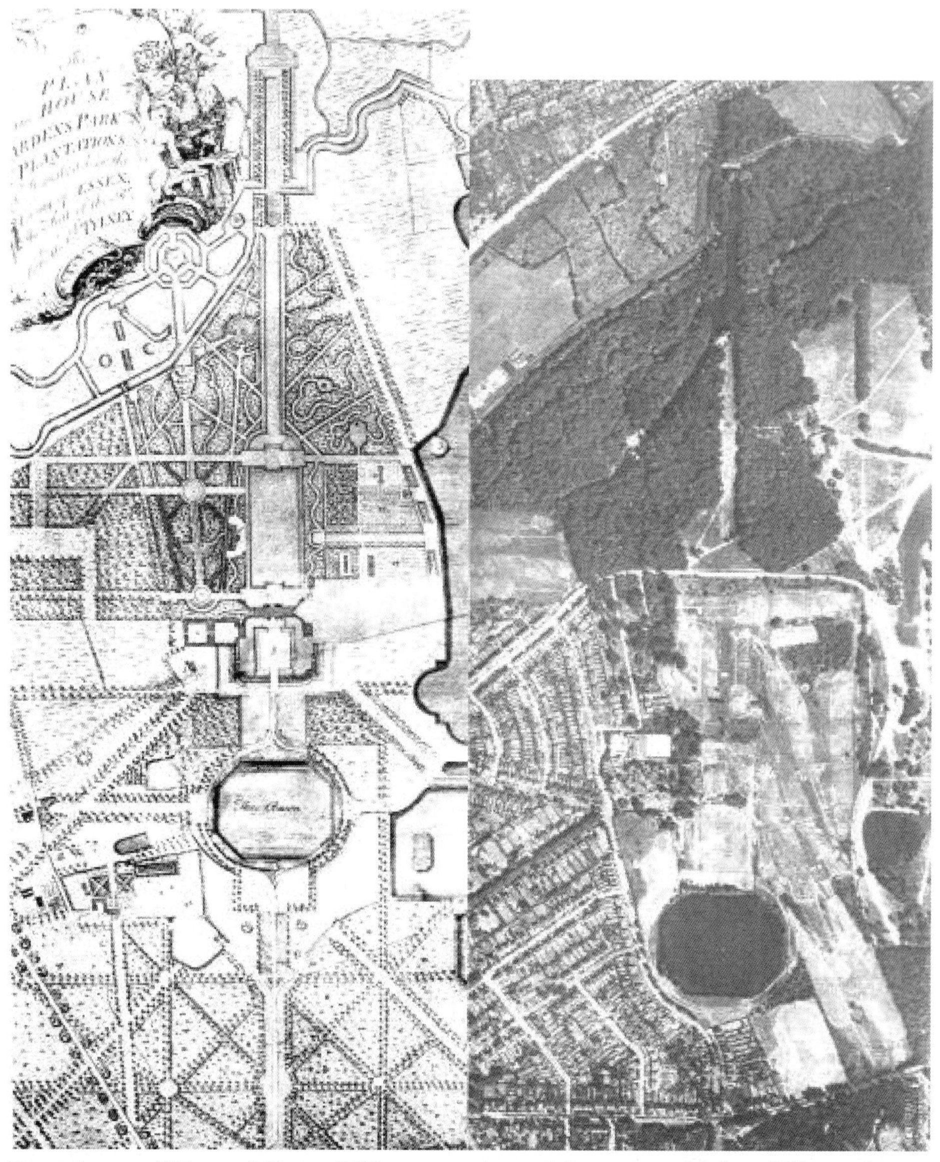

Rocque's map of Wanstead House, 1735
(Reproduced by courtesy of the Essex Record Office)

A twentieth century aerial view of Wanstead

The footpath to the grotto, Wanstead House (Reproduced by courtesy of the Essex Record Office)

The Lake House, Wanstead Park (Reproduced by courtesy of the Essex Record Office)

If Wanstead House was one of the grandest gardens in Essex, then the 8th Lord Petre must be considered the greatest gardener! Robert James, 8th Lord Petre [d. 1742] was born in 1713, he was a posthumous only child, his father having died of smallpox. From an early age Petre was interested in gardening, planting sweet chestnut seeds that attained a height of 20 feet by the time he was 27. This interest was probably nurtured by his grandmother Mary, widow of the 6th Baron, who was a keen gardener; after her death in 1730, an Ingatestone Hall inventory lists the plants in her greenhouse, that included orange trees, yellow Spanish 'Jessamines' and myrtles. Petre even had his own gardener as a child. Whilst still young Petre became acquainted with Philip Miller, the keeper of the Chelsea Physic Garden and the pioneer in hot house germination of seeds. Another great influence of Petre was Philip Southcote, son of his guardian, Sir Edward Southcote. Philip together with William Kent had the greatest influence on the change from formal garden to natural landscape.

By 1730, at the age of 17, Petre had completed his Tour of the continent and built up an impressive botanical and gardening library, a year later he was elected a Fellow of the Royal Society. John Martin who was his sponsor for the Royal Society visited Petre in 1731 to see his 'stoves'; these hothouses were said to be the largest probably in the world and stood 30 foot high, 60 foot in length and 20 foot in width and Martin had never seen such plants as were grown in them: limes, bananas, guavas, papyas, passion fruit, pineapples and ginger.

At the age of 18, Petre married Anne Maria Barbara Radcliffe, daughter of the 3rd Earl of Derwentwater, and planned to rebuild Thorndon Hall and landscape the grounds; for this he employed the architect Giacomo Leoni and the surveyor Sieura Bourguinon. The grand plan of Bourguinion was never to reach fruition.

Petre was already a collector of plants before his wonderful gardening association with Peter Collinson and John Bartrum. He had acquired plants from voyages of Mark Catesby, who was collecting between 1712-26 for another Essex gardener, Samuel Dale, the apothecary from Braintree, amongst others.

Petre probably met Collinson, a haberdasher, at the Royal Society or he may have had business dealings with him in the course of rebuilding Thorndon Hall. Collinson had become associated with Bartrum, a farmer, through a mutual friend Benjamin Frankland. Bartrum although ill-educated was fascinated with plants and later created the first American Botanical Garden on his farm at Kingssessing Creek, Pennsylvania.

Collinson's enthusiasm for plants turned his hobby into a business and he became one of the first great commercial seedsmen. Collinson and Petre became very close despite the former being a Quaker and the other a Catholic, and Collinson was a regular visitor to Thorndon; on one such visit in 1733, he refers to Lord Petre's 'great Rowler for Rowling the Park'. Its diameter was 7 feet 7 inches, breadth 10' 2" and it weighed 11,750 pounds. It was drawn by two horses, or four if working all day.

The grand plans for Thorndon included leasing more land from the Duke of Kent for making an avenue of trees across Shenfield Common to Thorndon

Hall; 181 trees were planted either side, 4 trees at the top, 12 trees in clumps in the middle and 6 at the bottom of the avenue. They were 15-20 year old trees, 40-60 foot tall and teams of 20 horses were needed to draw them, but the planting was successful, a feat in itself!

The octagon plantation was the nursery where all the New England seeds and plants were grown; these arrived annually in boxes from America. There were other nurseries north-east of the house.

In 1740, 4,970 trees were planted in the park, they had all been grown by Petre from seed in his nurseries, they included:

70 Pennsylvania cherries
76 Virginia flowering maples
59 Virginia acacias
69 Virginia tulip trees
230 Carolina oaks
1,185 Red Virginia cedars

M. Bourginon's plan for Thorndon Hall, 1733

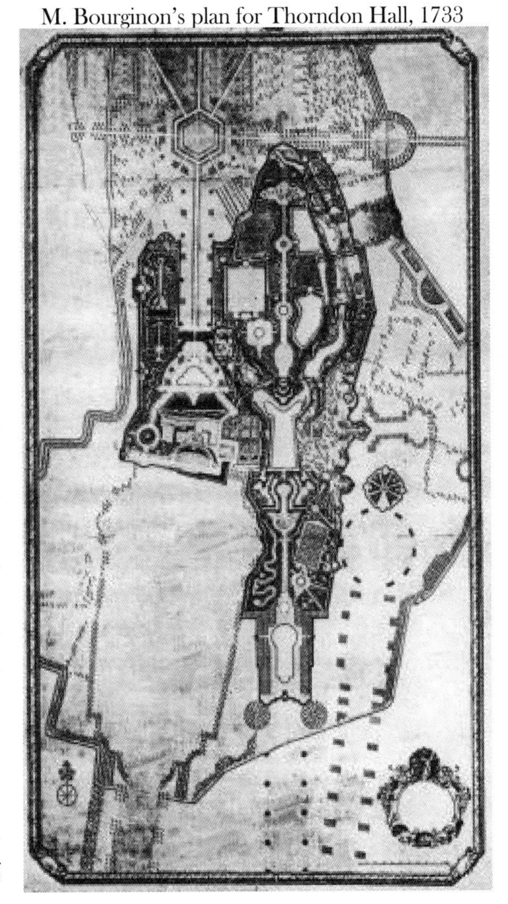

Collinson, writing in 1740, describes how Thorndon then looked: 'At Thorndon in Essex near Brentwood Lord Petre in the year 1740 finished the Esplanade on the Top of the Park and then Planted the Two Mounts which he raised att great Expence - the Mount near the new Church is Raised over the Ground about 91 feet high. The Tops of the Mounts are planted with a Cedar of Lebanon about 6 or 7 feet High and Twenty years old from Seed; there is four Smaller Ones on Each Side, the Great one that are about Two Feet high and Tenn years old - The Larix's about them are 3 feet High and Tenn years old. The Mounts are mostly planted with Red Virginia Cedars 3 years old being raised from seed from Pennsilvania with other Evergreens of His Raising. The Four Clumps of Larix on Each side of the Road next the park gates was then about 7 or 8 foot high and Tenn years old." The following two years, some 40,000 more were planted out [see page 71 for list]. It was the first extensive planting of North American trees in Britain.

Petre died aged 29 from smallpox, like his father before him. Collinson writing to Bartrum two years after his death still mourned him and wrote "the greatest loss that botany and gardening ever felt in this island". When he died, there were reckoned to be 219,925 plants in his nurseries, mostly exotics. Petre's imports are recorded in Hortus Siccus or herbarium, which extended to 16 volumes and 1,500 pages compiled around 1740. Eleven volumes are dedicated to Caribbean plants gathered by William Houstoun, ship's surgeon, two volumes on English plants, collected by Sir John Hill, an enthusiastic botanist and the remaining volumes are those collected by John Bartrum.

Collinson took over the responsibility for disposing of the plants in Petre's nursery; there was no lack of buyers! Lady Petre could not afford gardeners, but even so the trees matured to perfection, although not to everyone's taste; Horace Walpole visiting in 1754 found it all "the brobdingnag of bad taste', but most people were very impressed and by 1760 Collinson himself said the Virginia Red Cedars 'made an amazing fine appearance'. Thorndon could boast the finest trees in England and the greatest variety of exotics which had attained perfection never before known in this country. The ninth Lord Petre was also a keen gardener and was known to have purchased the ten-guinea boxes of American plants from Collinson. Collinson writing to Bartrum said 'It may truly be said that the spirit of Elyat rests upon Elisha'. Much of the 8th Lord Petre's work was destroyed when 'Capability' Brown landscaped the park for the 9th Lord. Collinson died in 1768, leaving Bartrum without his English connection, but a new patron was to replace Lord Petre; namely Dr. John Fothergill of Upton House, West Ham, he went on to deal with Bartrum's son William eventually. Bartrum was responsible for two-thirds of the 300 new plants that were introduced into England between 1735-80.

Dr. John Fothergill [1712-1780] was born in Wensleydale, Yorkshire, the son of a Quaker, and was as famous for his apothecary skills as his botany. He presumably met Peter Collinson through the Society of Friends. His first garden was in Surrey near the Thames, but this was not successful and in 1762 he purchased Upton House, West Ham with 30 acres, which he enlarged to 80 acres. Here he planted a Botanic garden, one of the finest gardens in England; only rivalled by Kew. Water flowed through the middle; the banks of which were planted with exotics. There were flower gardens surrounded by shrubberies and the wilderness area, full of trees from Bartrum and other collectors of the day included rare oaks, firs, maples, a ginkgo and Japanese maidenhair fern trees. His hot houses and greenhouses extended 260 feet from the house and contained oranges and myrtles amongst 3,400 other species from warm countries. The Arbutus Andrachna that differed from the common strawberry tree flowered for the first time in Fothergill's garden in May 1766; it grew to a height of 12 feet and after his death was sold for £53.11s. to a nurseryman.

He received the same annual boxes of seeds from John Bartrum and from his son William, also from another Pennsylvania man, Humphrey Marshall, cousin to Bartrum. The War of Independence stopped the trade. James Gordon, Lord Petre's former gardener, then owner of his own nursery at Mile End, also supplied Fothergill with plants. Gordon, whilst in the employ of Petre had procured a sucker of a single red camellia that had been sold to Lord Petre for a considerable sum, by Jesuit, George Joseph Kamel who had visited Japan in 1739. The two plants were placed unwitting in the hot houses where they died. Gordon's plant survived for 94 years in a conservatory.

Upton became a burden to Fothergill in later life and he only visited there on a Saturday. Fifteen men were employed in the gardens as well as three or four artists, recording the beauty of the plants. These paintings were sold on his death to Empress Catherine II of Russia for £2,300 and were said to number 2,000. After his death in December, 1780 at the age of 68 the contents of his garden were sold, the bulk of which went to a colleague, Dr. Lettsom of Camberwell, who listed all his hot house plants under the title of Hortus Uptonensis; it included no less than 68 species of mesembryantheumum. The house at a later date was enlarged and changed its name to Ham House, this was pulled down in 1872 and the grounds now constitute West Ham Park.

In 1720 David Gansel [d.1732] built Leyton Grange on the site of the previous house, to his own designs. The plans of the grounds, and this is all that is known about them, shows a very ambitious scheme, including converging avenues of trees and a forecourt flanked by outbuildings. The house lay on the line of the present Grange Road.

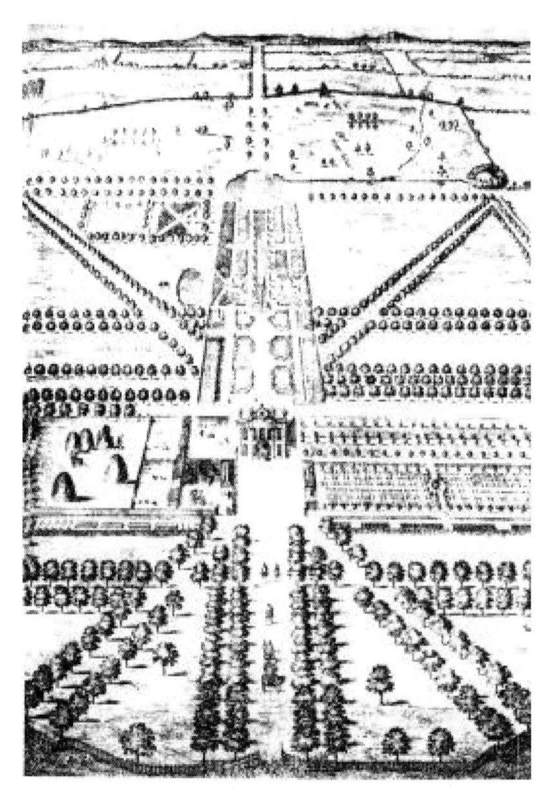

Leyton Grange, 1720, 'the seat of David Gansel Esquire who Design'd and Executed it himself'

Charles Gray acquired Colchester Castle together with Hollytrees House in 1726. The castle was in ruins, but was probably a focal point of his newly laid out park; the earthworks being used as a raised walk. The summer-house, still in existence, is in the form of a Greek temple and dated 1731, and a rotunda is dated 1747. He planted 2 Cedars of Lebanon, 2 Cedars of Bermuda and a cork tree. The Castle Park was declared a public open space in 1892.

Copford Hall had a thriving kitchen garden before Richard Woods created his master plan. Planting lists of fruit trees survive from 1730-50 with the date that the fruit trees were planted, the earliest date being 1690, when black and white sweet water grapes were planted next to the new parlour. The lists [see page 71] give an insight into the incredible amount of different varieties of fruit trees available at this time, far more choice than is available today. There are many gardening notes amongst these papers, which were made during the ownership of Copford Hall by Hezekiah Haynes [d. 1763]; Wallflowers to be sown at full moon in April; clay and horse dung to cure canker after cut off; Walnuts to be planted in green so that the mice will not eat them!

An engraving of 1735 shows the wonderfully elaborate layout of the gardens of Copped Hall in Epping prior to its demolition in 1748. There are also two paintings by George Lambert [1710-65], dated 1756, painted to record its appearance before demolition, giving rise to the issue of the date of its actual demolition!

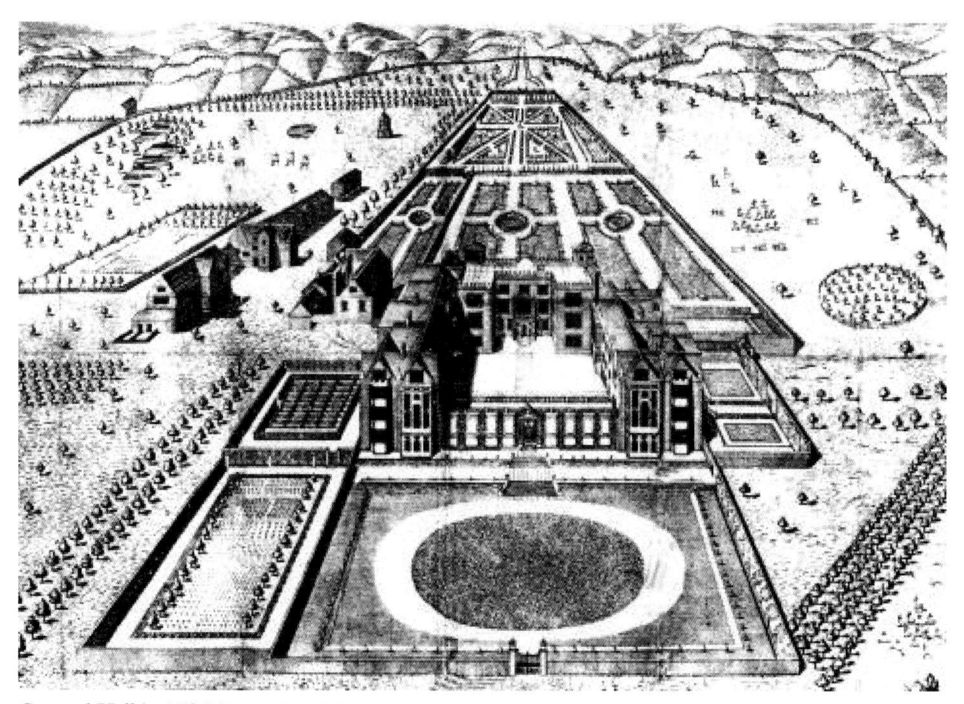

Copped Hall in 1735 (Reproduced by courtesy of they Essex Record Office)

A new house was built between 1751-8, for John Conyers; at the same time Conyers, with the assistance of Sir Roger Newdigate [1719-1806], was redesigning the gardens. There are various sketches, some no more than scribblings, showing a canal and lake, a menagerie, a scheme for planting with evergreens, a plan for the upper part of the warren to extend from the principal entrance to the gate of the 30 acre Copse Wood, and a ride through the wood, and a design for converting the old arcade into a magnificent ruin. A belt of trees was planted adjoining Raveners Farm including oak, ash, birch, hornbeam, hazel, aspen, and beech. Further trees planted in the park on 2 November 1751 included 123 elms, 4 arbrels and 2 thorns; in the lawns 7 thorns, 5 hornbeams and 1 oak, and in the Walk 41 arbrels, 1 ash and 1 hornbeam. There were a total of 196 trees planted at 6d. a tree.

A small temple in the gardens of Copped Hall

Gosfield Hall had extensive alterations after Robert Nugent [1702-88] married Anne Knight, widow, in 1736. The house was enlarged and the park improved by extending the lake to nearly a mile in length, with lawns running down to it. Writing to Sanderson Miller in 1748, Nugent said Gosfield Hall "is greatly altered, the lawns are greater, the water is greater, the plantations are much greater and the house indoors is hardly to be known again.' Walpole was also impressed with it, "the park is to be 1,600 acres ... the lake which is very beautiful is of 70 acres, directly in line with the house, at the bottom of a fine lawn.'

The landscape remains and several of the original tree plantations of Weymouth or Eastern white pines and scots firs were in existence in this century along with two of the cedars and a tulip tree in the Menagerie Plantation.

Gosfield Hall, 1837, showing the 'improved' lake.
Lithograph by J W Giles from a painting by H Strafford

Prior to the work we assume that Woods carried out at New Hall, there is a description of the land when it was conveyed from Benjamin Hoare, the younger son of Sir Richard Hoare, a rich banker in Fleet Street and Lord Mayor of London in 1713, to John Olmius of Little Leighs for the sum of £11,367.3s.4d. in June 1738. The estate consisted of:

1. The Mansion House called 'New Hall', with the green enclosed with pales, and houses, outhouses, edifices, buildings, barns, stables, courts, yards, gardens and orchard thereto belonging, containing 14 acres.

2. 2 plantations of firs, with the wilderness between them containing 18 acres.

3. A paddock of 6 acres adjoining the orchard.

4. The deer park 'called New Hall Park, where the deer are now kept, containing 591 acres with the stock of deer therein.'

5. The walk near the mansion house called Pall Mall Walk.

6. The long walk planted with limes [said by Morant to be one of the finest avenues of lime trees in the kingdom, about a mile long].

Bourginon, the French surveyor who had created the wonderful designs for Thorndon, reputedly made a less elaborate design for Weald Hall in 1738. As previously mentioned Weald Hall had a deer park in the 12th century, during the 16th century it was surrounded by a series of walled courts and gardens that included two garden houses in the same style as the Hall. One of these survives as a private house known as Queen Mary's Chapel, as it was reputedly the worshipping place of Mary I. The map of 1738 was never fully executed; it was centred on a stylised lake with straight avenues leading to temples on the higher ground to the north and south. The Belvedere Temple, so named 'beautiful view', and octagon in shape, was built by the time Hugh Smith died in 1745 and several avenues of chestnuts are evident from the plans, sloping from the mound north-westward. The natural hillside around the Temple was made into ornamental gardens, with an early example of a ha-ha at the foot of the slope to keep deer out. Thomas Tower bought the estate in 1752 and raised the height of the Belvedere Temple. Further work was carried out, as can be seen in the 1788 map.

Benjamin Mildmay, Earl Fitzwalter, bought Moulsham Hall with 45 acres for £630 from his sister-in-law, on the death of his brother, in 1728. It was a Tudor house, with a large garden walled on three sides on the south-west of the Hall and contained eight rectangular beds intersected by three paths in one direction and one across; a fountain stood in the centre.

Fitzwalter demolished the old Hall a piece at a time and rebuilt in a classical style, from plans by Giacomo Leoni. At the same time he was replanning the garden. In January 1730 Mr. Greening, the nurseryman, was paid £32.13s.8d. for plants supplied and 6 guineas for going down four times to Moulsham Hall to give advice. Another eight loads of trees arrived in April and by October Greening's bill was £171.19s. The kitchen garden walling commenced in 1731 by bricklayer Dick Eves, his bill of £94.10s.7d. was for 81 rod of walling. The bricks were produced by Thomas Spice; the first consignment being 101,300. By August of the same year a further 6 kilns had been fired. The walls were three bricks in depth. In 1733 Dick Eves was paid a further 10 guineas for the south-west end of the kitchen garden and on 27 May 1734 was discharged from his building. Fruit trees were brought from Paris to London for him in 1731; and in 1732 Alexander Horne, a gardener at Boreham, was paid £20 on account for making the Great Pond in Conduit Field. Flowers arrived from Richard Dobson of Clapham in 1734 that consisted of Dutch anemones, English anemones, jonquils, double pinks, carnations and polyanthus. Fifty-two large standard English elms came from Henry Hewett in 1735 followed by another fifty-two from Elizabeth Frazer of Brompton, nurserywoman; these were planted in the principal walk in the garden. A further forty standard elms and three hundred hedge elms arrived in 1738 from Edmond Bolton at Ilford for the new walk to the Perry Field; Bolton supplied further plants for that part of the plantation in the garden next to the mount in October 1740.

Extra garden labourers were needed for planting the standard elm trees in the principal walks in 1734. The following year, Fitzwalter discharged a gardener, one William Shenton, who was a very lazy, idle fellow, he was paid £11.15s., being seven months work at twenty pounds per annum: he was replaced by a Frenchman, Peter le Dean. Another gardener was discharged with no reason given; Richard Plater had been working additional hours following the death of Fitzwalter's steward, Dwinger. But Plater remained on good terms with Fitzwalter as he was renting a hop ground and public house from him. He was gardener from 1729-33 and received £20 a year and a house.

The demise of Moulsham Hall coincided with the Napoleonic Wars. The Mildmays were only living in the Hall for three months of the year, as was the obligation. Sir Henry thought the ideal way of ridding himself of this encumbrance was to lease the property to the government for the use of the

Garrison. This went ahead after repair work had to be carried out. The four year lease was not renewed. The house was now in a state of dilapidation and was pulled down in 1809.

An auction of the complete contents of the Hall took place on 6 March 1809, which even included selling the fruit trees and garden shrubs, followed by the demolition of the Hall itself; the garden house and walls were left standing. This area of 12 acres was recorded as the Great Wilderness on the 1843 Tithe Map and later as Moulsham Hall gardens. Between 1912-50 they were cultivated as a market garden by William Teager.

The Earl of Rochford's park and garden of St. Osyth's Priory was surveyed in 1762 by Edward John Eyre. The map shows parkland interspersed with copses, a wilderness garden, a stretch of water, and a kitchen garden. The park contained Lombardy Poplars, a fine avenue of limes and beeches leading to Nun's Wood, within the wood lay a grotto, the walls of which were adorned with shells. The garden changed little from 1762 to a map of 1814 and through to the Tithe Map of c.1840. Eyre, a London-based surveyor, had several commissions in Essex, including the whole parish of Epping for John Conyers of Copped Hall, but this did not include detail of the gardens. He also did a plan of Audley End house and garden in 1757.

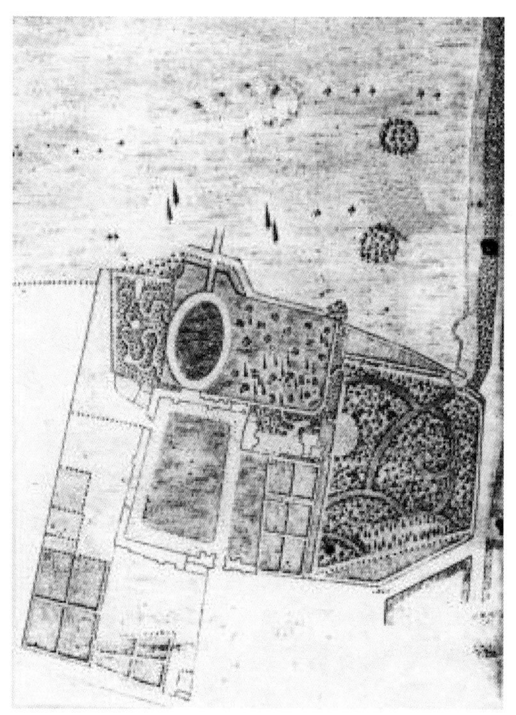

Detail of the garden of St Osyth's Priory from John Eyre's 1752 map

In 1766 John Mackoun produced a volume of maps for the vast estates of John Barrington of Barrington Hall. The 5,463 acre estate extended from Hatfield Broad Oak to Matching, Aythorp Roding, Stansted, White Roding and Takeley. They are beautifully executed drawings, the one relating to the Barrington Hall park shows deer in the park, swans on the lake, with gates, stiles, hedges and fences shown in detail. The parkland lay to the south of the house, with an approach from the south-west by an avenue from Feather Hill. There was an artificial lake near the house and an ornamental temple in the centre of the park. The house was remodelled in 1863 and statuary and a capital from the earlier house were used as garden ornaments. A terrace was built along the south front to reduce the height of the basement storey.

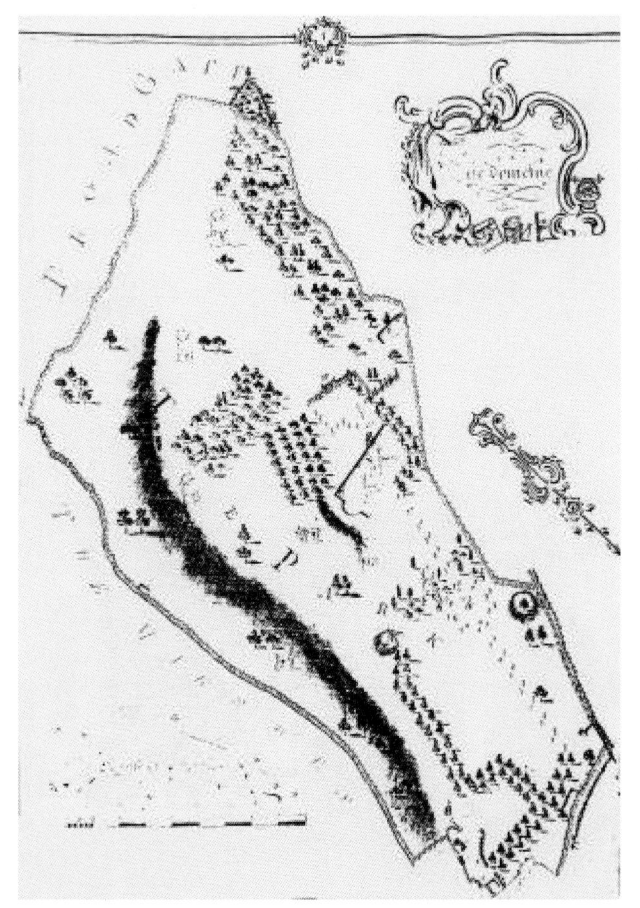

Barrington Hall, 176, by John Mackoun (Reproduced by courtesy of the Essex Record Office)

Work continued at Audley End right through the 18th century. In 1771 a three-arch bridge over the River Cam was built by Robert Adam [1728-92], who also designed the obelisk erected on a hill north of the house, in memory of the Countess of Portsmouth in 1774. In 1783 the Palladian bridge and tea house were built. At this period 50 gardeners were employed, 12 mowing every day to clear the seven-mile-long grass walks. Joseph Hicks was employed as supervisor during this period and received £4,000 between 1774-1781, this vast sum shows the amount of work being carried out even after Brown had left. In 1785 the chief kitchen gardener was receiving £50 a year and Martin Nockold, a nurseryman, was receiving the same. In 1792 the Temple of Concord was built east of the house and new garden walls were built in 1803. An exceptional gale in 1833 brought down 540 trees of the period of Brown's planting, and one of the fine cedars was blown down in 1916, a section from the trunk was made into a table that was placed in the temple.

Audley End

John Player, writing in 1845 said, "its internal grandeur and external beauties, replete with all the varieties of hill and vale, wood and water, are rarely to be combined in such limits ... Its palatial character, with its trees and gardens, is there very imposing and resting in quiet splendour amidst much agreeable scenery, it cannot fail to awaken admiration."

Today, those sentiments still apply, this is not one of our lost gardens, the landscape remains, but the flower gardens, designed by the 4th Lord Howard of Walden and his Lady have gone.

Thomas Warren's survey of Audley End, 1783 (Reproduced by courtesy of the Essex Record Office)

Chapter Four

The 19th and 20th Centuries

History - or should I say fashion - usually repeats itself, and so it is with gardening. The Tudor period with severe topiary parterres was replaced with vast landscape plantings. The 19th century returned to formal flower beds, the particular love of the Victorians, with the massed colours of annual flowers. The turn of the century brought the arts and crafts movement that returned gardening to a more 'natural' style. Hardy perennial plants were used instead of greenhouse raised annuals. There was more of a balance between house and garden, indeed the garden became the extension of the house. The terrace was used for tea, garden parties and garden fêtes abound. The Loggia replaced the Conservatory, rose-clad pergolas lead to arbours and summerhouses. Gardens were turned into 'rooms' some housing formal water gardens, each one to give a delight at every turn. Woodlands were planted with rhododendrons, azaleas and camellias, and rock gardens were constructed, some on a massive scale. This was the era of the partnership of Edward Lutyens and Gertrude Jekyll, who, alas, left no record in Essex; although Lutyens did plans for a cottage at Easton Lodge.

The 19th century was the era of the kitchen garden. Many exotic fruits and vegetables seeds were coming to this country, and the Victorians were certainly noted for the array of produce that could be grown in these kitchen gardens. Hylands House, near Chelmsford, was trying new methods of fruit growing with Dutch forcing ideas.

Hylands park: the 19th century greenhouses in the 1930s
(Reproduced by courtesy of Chelmsford Libraries)

After the death of Kortright in 1813, Pierre Caesar Labouchere [d. 1839] bought Hylands and made more changes in the garden. The green-house was replaced with a much larger erection of 250 feet in length, with Portland flag-stones and cast-iron hot water pipes. It was probably designed by William Atkinson [1773?-1839] who was the first inventor of practical apparatus for heating greenhouses. Labouchere bought new ideas from his continental travels, one of which was a cherry orchard, whereby the trees were protected by fishing nets specially made at Bridport, Dorset, supported by nine foot high wire fences; the area covered was one rod and twelve perch and contained 98 trees of the varieties May Dukes, White Hearts and Circasrain as well as gooseberries, red, white and black currants, raspberries and strawberries which were interplanted.

The Dutch method of forcing vegetables was pioneered at Hylands by one of the gardeners; Francis Nieman had been brought from Haarlem in Holland in 1824 especially for the purpose. He used dung heat in pits, leaf mould instead of loamy soil and reed mats for covering crops. The hot bed frames measured 9'6" x 6'3" with two sashes. For lettuce it was divided into 30 squares, for other crops 42 squares. This method allowed cucumbers to be cut every month of the year. Melons were cut as early as May and beans could be produced throughout the winter. There were 8'6" pits surrounded by brick walls for peaches, apricots, vines and raspberries. Apricots were picked at the end of April and peaches the second week in May.

The Horticultural Society of London awarded Labouchere the Banksian Medal on 25 May 1832 for his exhibit of forced apricots, raspberries, and melons, and again on 10 May 1834 the silver Banksian Medal was awarded for forced apricots and raspberries. He also exhibited at the Chelmsford Horticultural Show.

By the time Arthur Pryor bought Hylands in 1858 for £45,000 the acreage had been reduced to 843 acres; the previous owner, John Attwood, had added several hundred acres to the estate, but went bankrupt and the land was reclaimed. Pryor made many changes, demolishing the walls surrounding the vegetable and flower gardens to the north of the house and building a gardener's bungalow of brick and slate, which was occupied by Mr. Bowman. A description of the garden appears in the Gardener's Chronicle of 11 June 1881 under his care. "The garden was covered with mysotis, wallflowers, silene and spring bedding plants. In the flower garden 1,000 Belvoir Castle and Tom Thumb wallflowers were planted, 2000 Mysotis Dissitiflora, daisies in great numbers of red and white, Aubretia Purpurea, large beds of yellow violas and Cliveden purple pansies, with masses of Pilene Pendula Compacta, Bougainvillea grown to perfection, and Lapageria Alba, gloxinias, calceolarias and pelarganiums graced the greenhouses."

In the kitchen garden of 8 acres were 16 houses for fruit, 4 vineries and 2 small vineries, a house for french beans also containing an Osborris Prolific fig in a pot, 3 peach houses, 2 pineries, 2 melon houses and 2 houses for strawberries, and an apple orchard of 4 - 5 acres.

The next owner, Sir Daniel Fulthorpe Gooch leased Hylands from Pryor for a year before buying it in 1907. There were between 16 - 20 gardeners at the time, Harold Fairbank, O.B.E., one of the gardeners, started work there whilst studying at the County Institute at Rainsford End gardens. The large greenhouse, presumably Atkinson's, now consisted of a large Palm house, a tropical house, and a temperate house. Malmaison carnations were grown by William Heath, who later as W. Heath and Sons, became suppliers of dianthus plants. His skills were passed to Harold Fairbank, who accompanied the Head Gardener when displaying at the Royal Horticultural Halls in Vincent Square, London, where they were awarded a silver gilt medal.

The last private owners were the Hanbury family: Mrs. Hanbury planted the rhododendrons and made the greenhouse into a covered swimming pool Some time after her death on 12 May 1962, the Chelmsford Borough Council bought the house and grounds of about 428 acres as a public park for the people of Chelmsford.

Another garden noted for its orchards in the early nineteenth century was Glazenwood in Bradwell-juxta-Coggeshall. The inspiration behind this was Samuel Curtis a noted florist. Curtis [1779-1860] was born into a Quaker family, and his first garden of some importance was at Walworth, Surrey. In 1801 he married the only daughter of his cousin William Curtis [1746-99], author of Flora Londoniensis and founder of the Botanical Magazine in 1787, to which Samuel succeeded after William's death. He published his Beauties of Flora in 1806 with coloured plates of flowers drawn from his collection by two artists of repute, Thomas Baxter [1782-1821] and Clara Maria Pope [d.1838], and a monograph of the genus Camellia. He rented Glazenwood in about 1805 with 50 acres of land and started his orchards. Writing in 1808 to the Society of Arts, who awarded him a Silver Medal for his work, he explained his method of planting apples and pears alternately with two rods apart, in rows which were then interspersed with rows of cherries, the whole area, while they were small, was then under-planted with vegetables, whose crops paid for the trees. Twenty or thirty years later, the cherries were removed to give ample room to the apples and pears. He also planted in another part of the orchard medlars, quinces, plums and walnuts. In 1808 there was a total of 4,620 trees. The orchard had 10,000 trees at its peak and also included peaches, nectarines, figs and soft fruits.

He also planted Dutch flowering bulbs, 600 varieties of roses, dahlias, tree peonies, and many herbaceous perennials and had an Australian and an American garden. In 1819 he purchased the property from Joseph Greenwood who had had the house built in 1803. Curtis held annual floral fêtes that drew thousands of people, canvas stabling was said to provide cover for 5-600 horses at these events.

In 1847, he retired to Jersey, and Sir John Page Wood, vicar of Cressing, acquired the property. His daughter, Anna Steele wrote a novel based on Glazenwood called Gardenhurst published in 1866 in three volumes. She mentions Curtis in it: "He brought flowers from every part of the world to this his great altar to Flora, he imported rhododendrons from India, azaleas from America, tulips from Belgium, peonies from Persia, and slips and cuttings of every description from all the best nursery grounds in England." It had many owners after Curtis, including a commercial nursery that produced the most hot-house peaches in the country, supplying London restaurants and even the Cunard Liners. The garden became neglected by the 1950s, until the present owners made it come to life again. The magnificent orchards, of course, have gone, but an avenue of pear trees remain and there are rhododendrons and azaleas in the woodland, probably of Curtis's planting, and the semi-circle of mature limes to the east of the forecourt is probably of his time.

Birch Hall was rebuilt by Charles Round in the mid-19th century, designed by Thomas Hopper [1776-1856]. An earlier map of 1800 surveyed by W. Cole, for James Round shows canal, plantations, greenhouses and orchard and a Scotland plantation. Scant references are made to the garden in Charles Round's diaries, but on the morning of 9 December 1846 "the first Levant Oak was moved up by his machinery on the lawn and there planted.' Ten years later William Andrews Nesfield was called in to give advice, which must have been critical according to the diary entry for 10 April 1856, "Something may come of his visit: he pointed out our mistakes and our mismanagement very clearly." The plans arrived on 14 August 1856.

Nesfield [1793-1881] was asked by the Rebow family to devise plans for Wivenhoe House garden in 1847-8, and had advised on entrances and carriage drives. This would have been at the same time as Hopper was altering the house. The Rebow family had escaped to Italy to avoid the rebuilding work. William Gurdon, presumably in the employ of the Rebows, writing to them in November 1847, tells of the progress: "Bowers and I set out the Eastern Entrance, from the front door, to where it falls on Nesfield's Hill. We have also set out the plantation on the new Park and have selected evergreens from Cant's for the Park. [This was newly acquired land from Nicholas Corsellis lying on the western side of the Park] The rare plants such as ilex, cypress, bays and red cedars, I shall stand at a distance."

Wivenhoe Park, 1816, by John Constable (Reproduced by permission of the National Gallery of Art, Washington)

Gurdon again writing in February, 1848, says "Much labour has been bestowed in planting out the gardens." In April 1848 an estimate was sent in for the Garden wall [the ha-ha as it is today] Four feet high on the lower side, it was built with red brick on two course footings, two feet were one and a half bricks in thickness, the remaining two feet one brick thick, pointed in blue mortar. The rate charged was 13s. per yard exclusive of digging. The moulded Portland cement used for the coping was 4s.1d. per yard. D. W. Coller's The People's History of Essex, 1858, gives a description of Wivenhoe Park after Nesfield had been here.

"The Park, which contains 250 acres, is entered from two lodge gates from the Colchester and Wivenhoe side, and affords fine picturesque and diversified views of hill and vale and woodland scenery, with prospects of Colchester and the surrounding country. From the principal entrance is a carriage drive, which in its gradual descent past a lake on the left, brings the house into view through an opening in a row of tall and venerable trees, bringing the margin of a broad sheet of water on the northern side. The Park, which has a fine herd of deer, is richly clothed with timber, and its forestal aspect and undulations towards the western valley, contrasting with the smooth and green lawn on the south, present a pleasant rural picture."

A map of 1758, commissioned by Colonel Thomas Ffytche and drawn by Joseph Dawson, shows the boundaries of Danbury Park, little changed from medieval times to the present day. The house at this date stood to the west of the present house. Two parallel avenues met in the courtyard on the north side. Another avenue approached from Riffhams Lane and another from where the lower lodge is. The south-east corner of the park was heavily wooded, with avenues radiating from Mount Pleasant Grove. The formal gardens lay to the east of the house, surrounded on two sides by a moat. In 1769 the park was said to be well stocked with deer.

In 1831 John Round purchased the estate and pulled down the old house and built a new residence in Elizabethan style, said to be one of the most notable houses to be built in Essex in the 19th century. The park and grounds were also remodelled at this time. One hundred and fifty oaks were brought from Round's manor at West Bergholt and American plants were ordered from a Chelmsford Nursery for the new American garden that lay to the north-west of the lake.

A sale catalogue of 1892 gives a good description of the 284 acres of park and pleasure gardens. "The pleasure grounds are celebrated for their beauty and luxuriance in specimen Coniferae and flowering shrubs. They comprise lawns, ornamented with flower beds, and adorned with weeping birch, copper beech, Cedar of Lebanon, silver fir, araucaria, deodora, Turkey oak, scarlet thorn, cupressa and acacia; also a sunk fernery with winding walk and running stream, a charming American garden [in a dell] with choice rhododendrons and azaleas in great variety, and a weeping willow. A Terrace walk in front of the Palace leads to the three sheets of ornamental water, fed by springs from the hills. There was a walled kitchen garden covering an acre, an outer garden, herbaceous borders and an orchard."

The house is now used as a conference centre, but public access is allowed to the lakes and parkland.

Weald Hall estate was considerably enlarged by the 1860s, and the new land was planted with conifers and beech, the chestnut avenue north-east of the lake was also planted in the second half of the 19th century. The fallow deer that had been in the park since the medieval period had red deer added to their numbers c.1870 and a small herd of Japanese sika deer as well as two Indian zebus cattle. In 1823 the silken-haired Kashmir goats had been imported, and were so admired by the visiting King George IV, that the Tower family presented him with some in 1828 that formed the basis of the famous herd in Windsor Great Park.

Belvedere Tower, Weald Park (Reproduced by courtesy of the Essex Record Office)

The conifer plantation was felled during the Second World War, and the war in general led to the demise of Weald Hall. The park had been requisitioned for troops, who breached the fences, which led to the escape of the deer after 700 years. The house became derelict and Christopher Tower decided to sell almost the whole estate of 2,000 acres to the Metropolitan Railway Country Estates Company in 1946, the County Council having lost the chance to secure the land for Metropolitan Green belt. The house was demolished in 1950. In 1952 the Metropolitan Railway Country Estates Company tried to sell the timber, but Essex County Council placed a timber preservation order on the park, and after rapid negotiations purchased the land in 1953 for £27,000. The Belvedere Temple and the stable block remained at this time, but were considered a safety hazard and thus demolished, but the landscape remains as Weald Country Park for all to enjoy.

Braxted Park was undergoing alterations to the grounds in the 19th century. This was another medieval deer park, in 1708 described as a 300 acre park stocked with 200 deer. The warren still existed; there were hay meadows, woods, a river with ponds and good gardens well planted with excellent fruit and vegetables. By 1751 the new owner Peter Du Cane had rebuilt the house, but it was his grandson of the same name who altered the grounds. During 1825-33 a four and half mile wall was built enclosing the park. A lake was made by damming the river, which had previously fed the old stew ponds, and a bridge was built across the eastern point. An elaborate ice house was erected near the lake and many exotic ornamental trees were planted. Recent restoration of the gardens has been taking place.

Pyrgo Park in Romford, was built in 1851-2 to the designs of Anthony Salvin [1799-1881] and was of Italianate design. M. Browne, writing during Victoria's reign, recounts his image of Pyrgo: "By separate fancy lodges the park is entered, and the house approached by north and south drives of upwards of a mile in length, and bounded by a line of old and ornamental timber ... The undulating park posses many walks and drives, which are made additionally pleasing by a constant change of scenery ... Adjacent to this farm are the extensive kitchen gardens and forcing houses, at the back of which an orchard stands, where traces of the palace moat are to be seen ... [This refers to Havering Palace].

Pyrgo Park

"Returning to the pleasure grounds, the first part I would mention is that called the 'Wilderness', which has recently been opened out and tastefully arranged in sylvan glades and vista walks, which lead to ferneries and summer seats beneath the aged oaks mentioned in my memoirs of old Pyrgo.

"Immediately about the house are gardens, walks and tennis lawns, su unded with broad terraces, raised and protected from the park by ornamental balustrading, supporting vases at its various buttresses.

"This plateau or Italian garden was designed in 1863 by Edward Kempe, a land-scape gardener at Birkenhead. Descending from these terraces on which the mansion stands, we reach the slopes, the fernery, the island and the lake which wends its way beneath the bridge, hiding its course in distant shrubberies. This is the feature of most recent date, designed and executed by Henry Vine, the present steward of the park."

The house was demolished c.1940, but the Victorian gardens were surviving c.1980, the terrace having been partly excavated during 1972.

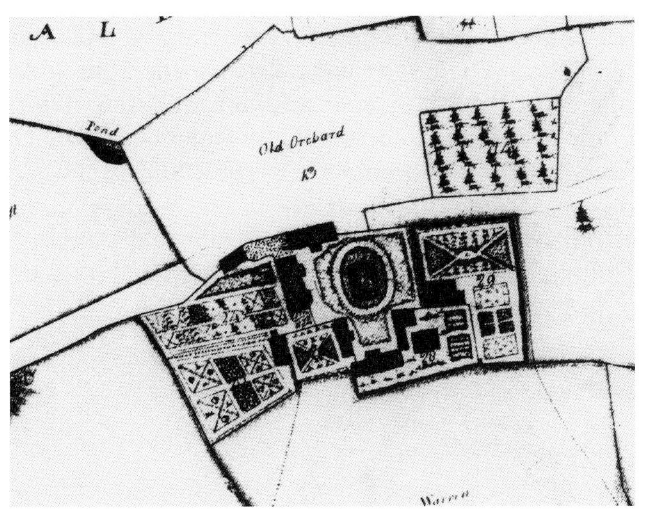

Hassobury, 1778 (Reproduced by courtesy of the Essex Record Office)

Hassobury in Farnham was a Domesday manor, but nothing is known about the gardens until a map of 1778 that gives a beautifully laid out formal garden, typical of an earlier period. This was all destroyed when the house was rebuilt in the late 1860s, at a cost of £50,783.9s.3d. The gardens alone had £4,673.10s. 9d. spent on them in about 1871, and previous accounts for the terrace steps and walks in 1869 amounted to £1,310.15s. The accounts give a unique insight into the building of a 19th century kitchen garden with detailed building specifications for all the walls, greenhouses and boiler houses etc. In March 1871 garden walks, glasshouses and forcing pits were contracted for £1,330. Glasshouses alone costing £1,611 with the total bill including ground work amounted to £3,366, while the modest gardener's cottage cost £264.10s.9d. There was also a fruit room and a mushroom house. Other houses built in the kitchen garden were: two peach houses and a vinery at £372; an early peach house and vinery at £372, a late vinery at £553, lean-to pits at £192, two half span forcing houses at £472 each; a span forcing house at £372.10s. and two boilers totally £80.

Robert Marnock [1800-89] of London drew up the plans for the kitchen garden and pleasure garden surrounding the house. A ha-ha was built around this at a cost of £139 10s. and a further £250 was spent on the pleasure grounds. Marnock's expenses were £476.5s.11d. The kitchen garden to the north of the house measured 250' x 320', outside the walled area, near the gardener's cottage was an area for the growth of seakale, rhubarb and an asparagus bed. It was estimated that 350,000 bricks were needed in the 14" thick garden walls and greenhouse bases.

There are a not a lot of detailed planting plans, but the plantation near the house had 8 cedars interspersed amongst 450 scots larch, acacia, laurels and shrubs, and 3 plants of Salisburia adjantifolia placed 6-9 feet apart, together with 3 lombardy poplars placed 6-9 feet apart. There was also a plantation of cedars north-east of the house. The house and walls near the house were covered in various ivies supplied by Paul's Nurseries at Waltham Cross. The lists consisted of 34 different varieties, 16 green forms and 18 variegated. The green varieties cost 1 shilling each, 10s.6d. a dozen, or 75s. per 100, and the variegated ones were 1s.6d. each, 15s. a dozen or £5 for 100.

During the 1920-30s there were seven gardeners and two boys, and a pony cart took fruit and vegetables to Bishop's Stortford Hospital twice weekly.

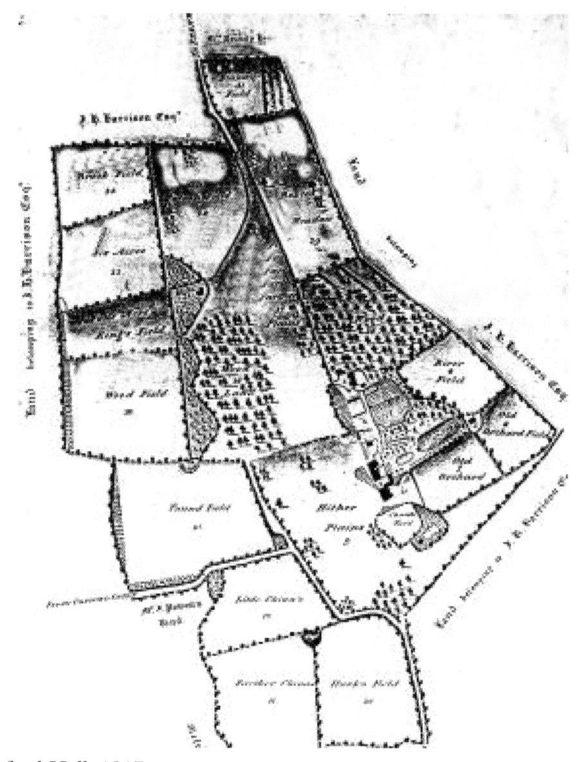

Copford Hall, 1817 (Reproduced by courtesy of the Essex Record Office)

Copford Hall had been in decline when Thomas Haynes Harrison, nephew of Fiske Harrison took on the estate after the death of his uncle in 1872; he had been farming in New Zealand for twenty years. A quote from a contemporary paper recorded his arrival, saying "the Hall has been closed to the public for a quarter of a century, and that under its previous owners Major Harrison, Copford Hall was noted for its hospitality as well as the beauty of the grounds, covered with magnificent Oaks, Cedars, and other trees, and varied by several prettily laid out ponds of water, and an adjacent rivulet..."

Whilst the Hall had been empty a gardener called David Prior was the tenant, hiring the hot houses. It was this enterprising man who went on to found the well known Colchester firm of rose growers called Priors.

Easton Lodge emanated from a medieval deer park covering 1,000 acres. A map exists of 1730 showing an elaborate garden layout around the house with avenues of trees leading from the house right through the parkland; these can still be seen on the 1876 6" Ordnance Survey map.

Easton Lodge: the flower garden in 1907 (Reproduced by courtesy of the Essex Record Office)

This garden, however, was at its zenith of glory when in the ownership of the Countess of Warwick [1861-1922] and her husband at the turn of the twentieth century. The Tudor house was destroyed by fire in 1847 and a new one built. The Earl of Warwick had an aversion to bare walls, and so clothed them to a height of 12 to 15 feet in various forms of ivy and elegant Ampelopsis Veitchi. The principal gardens were to the north of the mansion and were designed by Harold Peto at the turn of the century.

Harold Peto [d.1933] was born at Somerleyton Hall, Suffolk, into the large family of the building and railway magnate, Sir Samuel Morton Peto [1809-89]. Somerleyton itself was a lavish Italianate house surrounded by gardens designed by William Nesfield and Joseph Paxton [1801-65], which probably inspired the young Peto. He established an architectural partnership with Ernest George [1839-1922] in 1886, after training as an architect, and Edwin Lutyens [1869-1944] was one of their pupils. Peto modelled his work on the great Italian gardens, delighting in colonnades and statuary.

At Easton Lodge he created the sunken garden; this had a broad terrace on either side with a central lily canal, surrounded by borders; he also created a wonderfully elaborate rose clad arbour, made in the long out-moded construction of treillage (trellis-work). His design covered 10 to 12 acres of the parkland, and the work was undertaken by the Salvation Army Land Colony at Hadleigh, which was the first time they had attempted such work. There were 60 men working in gangs with three leaders, they were paid a daily rate and wooden buildings were erected for their accommodation. Lutyens designed the Easton Lodge Park cottages in 1900, presumably through his association with Peto.

Easton Lodge: the Italian garden in 1907, showing treillage on right (Reproduced by courtesy of the Essex Record Office)

Lady Warwick's great interest in gardening led her to establish a hostel for training women in those branches of horticulture for which they were suited. She also founded a school at Bigod, near Easton Lodge, to teach children farming and gardening. For several years she was president of the National Chrysanthemum Society.

Apart from the Italian garden, there was a rose garden containing between 6 and 7,000 plants. To the north of the Italian garden was a bosquet or wood, some two to three acres in extent, planted with limes in avenues, trained and cut to shape. Still north ward was the American garden, planted with heathers, azaleas, kalmias and other peat loving plants. The pleasure gardens were extended about 1905 from the American garden to the lake and ponds, and planted with broad borders and many ornamental trees, placed so as to give a glimpse of the lake with the ornamental Japanese tea house. The banks of the water planted with bamboos, polygonums, pampas grass, tritomas, Japanese and Siberian iris, spilobiums, arundas, senecios and lilies.

Another feature of much interest lay to the south-west of the park: Stone Hall, a small cottage with garden attached, it was the haven of the Countess after a season in London Society, writing in Lady's Realm in 1896, she takes one through the garden: "wander across the park with me, to the garden that I love, my playground, far from the busy haunts of men". It contained the Shakespeare border, through which many a winter evening had been spent hunting for quotations suitable for the plant labels representing doves; on one wing was the plant name, on the other the quotation. The Garden of Friendship contained plants as gifts from friends memorialised in heart shaped labels. The border of Sentiment was full of herbs and flowers, such as balm for sympathy, basil for hatred, bluebell for constancy, bay for glory, white clover, memory; foxglove, sincerity; yellow heartsease, waiting; heath and hemp for solitude and fate; blue salvia, knowledge; ear of wheat, intellect; veronica, fidelity and blue violet for love. The roserie was next, full of old fashioned roses. Verses were on Tudor rose labels telling of the love of the poet for the queen of flowers. A winding shrubbery led to the rock garden which contained too many treasures to mention - she continues: "You will weary of my Plaisaunce, and I will hold my pen, and only tell you that on yonder green slope, encircled by spreading chestnut trees, is my Lily garden with the quotations on labels of pottery fleur-de-lis, and round that old stone sundial, in reverent seclusion, is planted my garden of Scripture where beautiful thoughts will be written from the world's greatest book.

"But now the elms are beginning to cast vast shadows to eastwards, while the heavy scent of the honeysuckle tells us that the dews of evening are already claiming from it that frankincense with which it pays tribute to the night. As a further reminder, do we need it, that life for us both is a day older, there comes the harsh, long dawn 'gluck', 'gluck' of the blackbird in the laurels, begging that its roosting haunt may be freed from our presence. And so we will even fall in with the blackbird's lonely mood and wander homeward before the last of the bee tribe has winged its way to its hive, weary and heavy laden with the sweet burden of the summer's day."

Most of Easton Lodge was demolished in the mid-twentieth century, but some remains and the gardens are undergoing restoration.

Warley Place during the medieval period was the sanatorium of the Abbey of Barking, some of the remaining ponds were the medieval stew ponds. It later came into the hands of John Evelyn, the diarist, who owned it from 1649-55. It is said that the Spanish chestnuts, the walnuts and the crocus lawn are his plantings. He wrote Sylva in 1664, a discourse of forest trees, which remained the standard work on trees for over a century. He was also considered the father of the movement to plant ornamental trees and woodlands in our gardens

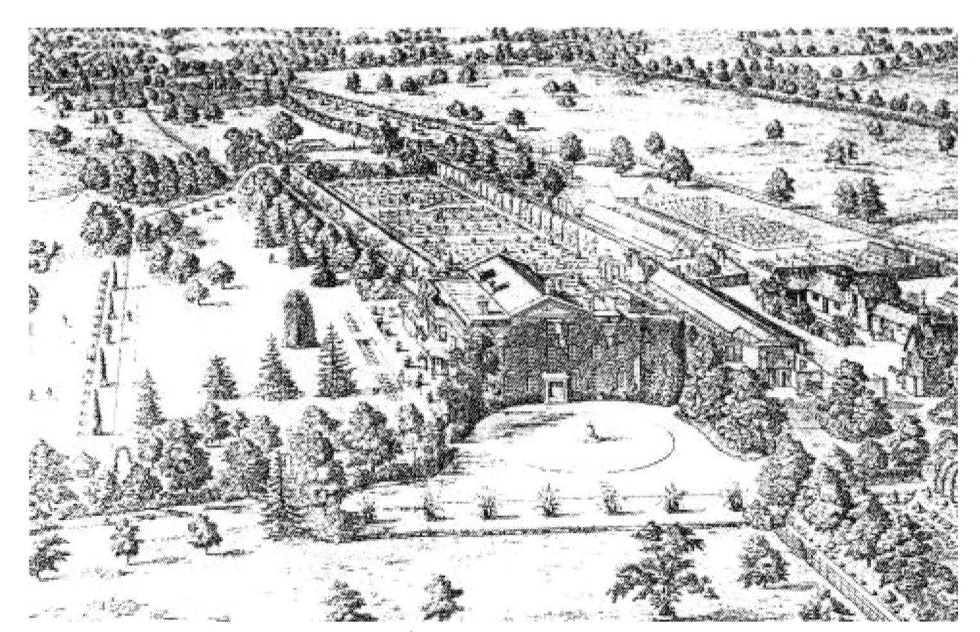

Warley Place and gardens in the early 20th century, looking west (Reproduced by courtesy of the Essex Record Office)

Warley Place: the south front

The real story of the Warley Place garden starts in November 1875, when Frederick Willmott bought the property with 33 acres; from the Sale Catalogue we have the description of the garden as it was before Ellen Willmott, Frederick's daughter, made it one of the most famous gardens of Essex in the early 20th century. "The pleasure grounds are very extensive, very tastefully laid out, and interspersed with a variety of trees and shrubs of luxurious growth. The kitchen gardens are of ample dimensions, partly walled in and provided with early and late vineries, greenhouse and cold pits."

Ellen, who was born 19 August 1858 at Spring Grove, Heston, Middlesex, where Sir Joseph Banks had earlier resided, took her love of gardening from her mother, and both Ellen and her sister, Rose, were excited at the move to Warley which gave them far greater scope than their previous garden. Within the year, Ellen was raiding the local gardens for all her favourite plants that were missing from Warley. Ellen must have been quite a character; Gladys Taylor, in The Victorian Flower Garden, says she was "ambitious, proud and beautiful, it is not possible to write so as to do justice to her complex personality. She was a woman of wealth and of many gardens, by turns munificent and mean. Her skill as a cultivator - and something of her vanity - is witnessed by the great number of plants that have been named after her, She was a capricious and implacable enemy, and a loyal friend."

Her first great achievement was the Alpine Garden; at the age of 21, having received £1,000 from her godmother for her birthday, she asked her father if she could create an alpine garden. Her father agreed, as long as it was not visible from the house. Frederick wrote in his diary 1 April 1882 'Ellie began her new alpine garden'. It took three years to build, James Backhouse and Son of York did the excavating and supplied the stone, which came from Derby. Henry Correvon, a botanist of Geneva, writing in 1905, gives us the best picture of what the alpine garden looked like; "It is not a ga4den; it is a valley hollowed in the mountains, and in this valley is shown a synthesis of the whole flora of mountainous regions. Plants of the Alps are side by side with those of New Zealand, plants of the Andes shelter those of Greenland, Kashmir is next to California, and the summit of Kilimanjaro joins hands with the heights of the Pamir. At the bottom of the valley runs a little stream; it murmurs a wild and plaintiff song. Hidden as one finds oneself among the masses of flowers, one feels as if transported into the midst of the great landscapes of Scotland or the Alps of Switzerland. The space occupied is over an acres, the valley runs from north-west to south-east, at the tower end is a lake that receives the stream after it has passed through a series of picturesque and well-planned gorges." Jacob Maurer, her alpine garden foreman, had been trained by Henry Correvon and arrived at Warley in 1894, from Switzerland. On the upper banks of this garden were alpine lawns for the smaller bulbs and halfway down a Fernery with a glass-covered fern house. The roadway ended at a pond near the entrance to the drive, set with aquatic plants and stepping stones.

Warley Place: border of hardy flowers, 1909. Ellen Willmott's own photograph
(Reproduced by courtesy of the Essex Record Office)

The alpine garden was but one area; to the north-east the land sloped westward from a broad terrace with a glazed summer-house, to a small, tree shaded, boating lake, with a landing stage and Swiss chalet, the margin of the lake contained an unrivalled collection of bog plants. Further north a group of heated glasshouses contained orchids, ferns, palms and other exotics. The walled garden approached from the herbaceous walk overlooked by the garden room, contained a wealth of rare perennials and flowering shrubs of great beauty and unusual variety, including a Camellia reticulata that had come as a cutting from Brighton Pavilion. Spring must have been magnificent with Magnolia Stellata under carpetted with chionodoxas and camellias on the north wall. A three-quarter acre old English garden, to the east of the north avenue contained a series of miniature rockeries, divided by flagged walks and intersected by box-edged plants. The Well Mead garden entered through a brick wall and timber gatehouse, contained a collection of rose species and older hybrid teas, one of the best collections of roses at this time. All these gardens were surrounded by park-like meadows planted with clumps of coniferous and other trees, underplanted skilfully with grouped masses of snowdrops, crocus and daffodil bulbs. One order alone was for 10,000 Cammassias to naturalize in the moist section of the parkland.

Warley Place: the Garden House, 1909. Ellen Willmott's own photograph
(Reproduced by courtesy of the Essex Record Office)

At the height of the garden's fame, there were said to be 104 gardeners, all equipped with uniform and green and cream boater hats, they included Swiss, Dutch, Italian and French gardeners, who all worked for a fixed weekly wage which never varied, the foreman of each section getting a trifle more. The gardens were visited by Royalty and well-known gardeners. There were said to be no fewer than 100,000 plants of varieties as well as species. Ellen had a card index of 30,000 plants, and could remember the names of 36,000, but her memory could contain no more! Her talents did not stop at creating the garden; she was hybridizing daffodils in the 1890s, and there were known to be 600 varieties of narcissus planted at Warley.

In 1894 she joined the Royal Horticultural Society, and was among the first women to be admitted to the Linnaean Society of London. Many plants were created and named by her, and many others named after her or Warley Place. Her unique collection of roses in the Well Mead garden led to the study and publication of The Genus Rosa published in two volumes in 1910 and 1914 and illustrated by Alfred Parsons [1847-1920]. She was also an accomplished photographer and produced her own book of photographs entitled Warley Place in Spring and Summer, published in 1909, which allows us an insight into the beauties of Warley Place.

Warley Place daffodils, March, 1998 (Photograph Wendy Stubbings)

Ellen had two other properties, Tresserve in Aix-les-Baines, France, and Boccenegra, Ventimiglia, Italy, which she visited every year, much to the consternation of her gardeners, as they had to correspond regularly by postcard telling Ellen what plants were flowering, or what they were doing. These all became a drain on her resources and neglect was creeping in by the time Ellen died in 1934. There was talk at this point of the gardens becoming a branch of Kew, but the project was dropped on the outbreak of the Second World War. The house and contents were put up for auction in 1935. Her library had at least 1,400 books on every aspect of horticulture.

Plans for a housing estate were submitted, but planning permission was never granted and the estate fell into decay. The house was demolished in 1939 and the land was subsequently leased to the Essex Wildlife Trust, whose members still have the pleasure of the great drifts of snowdrop, crocus and daffodil in their thousands every spring.

Marks Hall near Coggeshall has very ancient woodland on the estate and a 300 acre deer park, probably of medieval origin. The earliest pictorial evidence of the garden landscape is from a map of 1764 by Timothy Skinner that was commissioned by the then owner Lieutenant-General Philip Honywood, whose family had owned the estate since 1605. The map shows three lakes, the walled garden and a great avenue of trees to the north of the house. Richard Woods is supposed to have visited here en route to Wivenhoe, but nothing is known of any work he proposed. By the Tithe Map of 1842 the two smaller lakes have been formed into the present lower lake.

Marks Hall: restoration of the original garden (Photograph by Wendy Stubbings)

It was Philip Honywood who by his will forbade the felling of any of the park timber, especially the large oaks; Marks Hall had gained a considerable reputation for its fine park and woods. The Honywood family connection ended when considerable debts and a battle over inheritance ended in the Court of Chancery; the estate was auctioned in 1897.

The Sale Particulars give a good description of the estate. It was a deer park of 300 acres, containing majestic oaks of great size and age. There was a gardener's eight roomed cottage. The old walled kitchen garden was of 3 acres in extent with standard and wall fruit trees, asparagus beds and vegetable plot. There was a range of glasshouses, including vineries, peach house, tomato and cucumber houses and a rosary house. There were two stoke houses, potting sheds, potato stores and tool sheds. The lake supplied by natural springs rising in the park forming the source of Robins Brook which flowed right through the park and into the River Blackwater at Coggeshall.

The purchaser in 1897 was Thomas Phillips Price, originally from Llanarth in Wales, who inherited a fortune from his uncle Sir Thomas Phillips [1801-67], a solicitor who had invested wisely in coal bearing land in South Wales, and owned Llanellen Court in Monmouthshire, an estate of 300 acres. Thomas Phillips Price had been renting Skreens Park near Chelmsford before acquiring Marks Hall.

Thomas Phillips Price had no issue and wanted the estate to be left in its entirety to the Nation; the Director of Kew Gardens assisted him in making his will to that effect.

Unfortunately for Marks Hall he had not accounted for the Second World War or wife number three! She was much younger than him and, indeed, outlived him by 34 years. Price died in 1932 at the age of 88. By 1942 the Air Ministry requisitioned the mansion and large areas of land, moving Mrs. Price into a dower house on the estate. Earls Colne airfield was constructed on the land with all the association of roads and buildings that went with it. This, of course, led to the neglect of the whole estate and the mansion was vandalised. Mrs. Price had no desire to return there after the war and the house was demolished in 1950. With no appreciation for the land and no respect for her husband's will, she leased the deer park and woods to the Forestry Commission, after having already felled the magnificent park oaks that Honywood had done so much to save in the 18th century. Just one remains of these magnificent specimens for us to enjoy. Upon her death in 1966 a dilemma arose because of her husband's will, the land was now neglected and overgrown, but the Government decided a trust should be formed, and in 1971 The Thomas Phillips Price Trust was launched with the purpose of restoring Marks Hall to its former glory; the 18th century garden of the Honywoods. This is one 'lost garden' that can now be viewed as it really was, the walled garden, lakes, cascades and bridges have been accurately restored; a visitor's centre encourages the public to view, and a100 acre arboretum is to be created over the years, of specimen trees from most continents of the world spreading two miles along Robins Brook.

John Archer Houblon [d. 1891] extended the grounds of Hallingbury Place by enclosing part of Hatfield Forest. A map of 1853 shows a good landscape garden with plantations around the boundary called the Long Plantation, a lake in the centre of the park and a long tree-lined avenue to the house. His widow, Georgina Archer Houblon, writing in January 1892, wished to place on record the achievements of her husband before she had to leave the home she had had for 44 years. He had evidently loved the garden so much; he had built the conservatory and two lodges; he had made the flower garden with sunken fences surrounding it and planted the Cedar Avenue, with the alteration to the drive. The Orchard House, Vineries and Stove had been built by him. She goes on to say "the Deodars planted in the Elgin Coppice are from seed sent home from India by my cousin, the late earl of Elgin, we then changed the name of the coppice to Elgin, the plants have not done as well as we hoped.' The Jubilee Oak was planted 23 June, 1897, this survives in Morley's garden, an adjoining property. The trees and shrubs were cut down so as to give a view of the church and a seat was placed there for his benefit.

By 1910 the property was leased to Mr Lockett-Agnew, director of Thomas Agnew of London, Art Dealers. He was a very keen gardener and made many improvements, with the assistance of a Mr. Wallace. He redesigned the gardens, centering the main entrance on a T-shaped lily pool with flower beds and brick paths, surrounded by yew hedges.

The outdoor staff at Hallingbury Place about 1920

The half formal rose garden had a pergola extending the whole length, covered with pink rambler roses and pale blue clematis, which were repeated on the surrounding walls. Madonna lilies underplanted crimson roses, the whole being edged with lavender and grey-blue Nepeta Musinii. Tennis and croquet courts lay beyond. An ornamental pond lay to the right, its sloping sides planted with aquatic vegetation, and stepping stones led to the rock garden, where the water from the pond flowed through a chasm. A wild garden lay in another direction.

Hallingbury Place: a 19th century engraving (Reproduced by courttesy of the Essex Record Office)

The house was demolished in 1926, some of the building materials from Hallingbury Place were used to build Morleys, 200 metres to the west; the formal rose garden, tennis and croquet lawns now come in this property. The garden of Hallingbury Place remains to some extent, now part of the Water Garden Property, and Hatfield Forest now belongs to the National Trust.

A Country Life correspondent writing in 1902 claimed the Rose garden at Spains Hall, Finchingfield was probably the finest in East Anglia. This can be attributed to Mabel Ruggles, the wife of Archie, grandson of John. She moved to Spains Hall in 1894 from Durwards. Her favourite flower was the Rose. In a specially created garden with a sundial at its centre she planted Hermosa roses from Sir Walter Gilbey's vine-yards in France. Further rose beds flanked the walk in front of the summer house, and a rose-clad pergola spanning an old brick path, framed a perfect view of Boyton Hall through the trees. She also improved the kitchen garden to enhance the range of vegetables and fruit for elaborate dinner parties, in which she excelled. She had two beautiful china dessert services on which to display her produce of strawberries, raspberries, gooseberries, red and black currants, peaches, plums, figs, nectarines, pears, medlars, almonds, walnuts and filberts when in season.

Layer Marney Towers was undergoing major garden changes at this period. In the 1890s the Rev. Alfred Peache began to lay out a garden south of the gatehouse. By 1904 Walter de Zoete had acquired the property, he restored the buildings and established the main layout of the gardens using imported Italian sculptures.

Layer Marney Towers

Copped Hall completely changed its appearance at the end of the 19th century, when Ernest James Wythes [d. 1949] succeeded his grandfather as owner in 1887, after his brother George died without issue. He altered buildings and had the gardens reconstructed. Most of the garden design is attributed to Charles Eamer Kempe [d. 1907], who was better known as a stained glass designer and maker. The garden, of Renaissance style, lay to the west of the house, with a central east-west 'causeway' with fountain basins and north and south pavilions built of stone. It contained parterres, geometric beds and ribbon borders, with statues of Pan carved from Travertine stone surrounded by three dancing boys in bronze, and the statue 'Olympian Courtship'.

In 1910, probably at its zenith, the summer shrubs included cistus and Romneva Couteril, which has immense elegant pure white poppy-like blooms. Roses and clematis clad the walls, with bush roses filling the beds, along with endless displays from the herbaceous borders. The walls gave shelter for the winter evergreen shrubs of Choisya Ternata and Azara Microphylla, with forsythia heralding the spring. The park could be cleverly viewed through holes cut in the yew hedge on the northern boundary, which was planted with oaks, cedars and plane trees. The lawns towards the north gave way to a yew enclosed rose garden and bowling green.

The house was gutted by fire in 1917; the Wythes family moved to Wood House, about a mile east of Copped Hall, which had been built for a relative, and also designed by C. E. Kempe. The garden structure of Copped Hall remains, but completely overgrown and neglected, hopefully to be restored one day.

The gardens of Copped Hall (Reproduced by courtesy of the Essex Record Office)

A 17th Century Seed List

Bill of Theophilus Hampton, gardener 9 Feb. 1649.

Theophilus Hampton had been to London and purchased a bundle of reeds, 2 melon glasses, three cupping glasses and four baskets. He then went to Mr. Anthony Tyler's druggist shop in Bucklersbury in the City of London and bought the following seeds:

2 lbs	carrots	3s. 0d.	2 oz.	succory	4d.
2 1bs	onions	7s. 0d.	2 oz.	sweet fennel	2d.
1 lb.	parsnips	1s. 0d.	2 oz.	caraway	3d.
2 lbs.	radish	2s. 0d.	2 oz.	coriander	3d.
1 lb.	spinach	1s. 4d.	2 oz.	anise	2d.
1 lb.	lettuce	2s. 8d.	2 lb.	parsley	1s. 4d.
1 lb.	curled endive	1s. 2d.	2 oz.	chervil	1s. 4d.
1 lb.	long turnips	1s. 2d.	4 oz.	leek	1s. 0d.
1 lb.	round turnip	1s. 2d.	2 lb.	french fennel	1s. 4d.
1 lb	yellow turnip	1s. 0d.	2 oz.	winter savoury	3s. 0d.
4 oz.	beets	1s. 0d.	2 oz.	marigolds	6d.
4 oz.	asparagus	1s. 0d.	2 oz.	curled cress	4d.
2 lb.	kidney beans	1s. 2d.	2 lbs.	onions	1s. 0d.
1 oz.	cauliflower	6s. 6d.	4 oz.	black radish	1s. 4d.
2 qts.	sugar peas	4s. 6d.	1 oz.	dill	4d.
4 oz.	cucumber	1s. 4d.	2 oz.	pomoyones [pumpkin]	6d.

E.R.O., D/DP A170

From: Jeffers, R.M. 'A 17th Century Seed List' [The Herb Grower Vol. xix, no. 4. 1967]

Trees planted at Upper End of Park, May 1740 and on the two Mounts at Thorndon.

390 Horse Chestnut	161 Weeping Willow	331 Spanish Chestnut	45 Sweet Willow
208 English Elms	85 Striped Sycamore	60 Purging Buckthorn	140 Sycamore
34 English Maple	124 Occidental Planes	201 English Oaks	6 Striped Elms
70 Pennsylvania Cherries	25 Dutch Elms	60 Aria Theophrasti	100 White Thorn
290 Larches or	2 Double flowering Thorn	1500 Laurels	107 Black Walnuts
109 Cockspur Thorn	58 Ashen Leaf Maple	69 Virginia Tulip Tree	250 Birch
870 Hornbeam	230 Carolina Oaks	736 Hazels and Philberts	50 Manna Ash
1494 Scots Pines	42 Striped Sallow	32 Standard Yew	59 Virginia Acacia
50 Selecia Pines	327 Abeila or White Poplar		255 Boxhill Pines
747 Black poplars	10 Balm Gilead Firs	233 Black Cherries	112 Spruce Firs
25 English Walnut	63 Silver Firs	196 Limes	198 Ruff Yews
266 Beech	6 Stone Pines	50 Flowering Ash	10 Swedish Junipers
12 Cedars of Lebanon on Mount		604 Red Cedars on lower Mount	
562 Red Cedars on upper Mount		19 Red Cedars in clumps	

Besides these, 15,052 trees were taken out of the Woods and from the Plantations.

Gidea Hall

D/DBe E4 13 September 1793

Richard Benyon, Esq. with Solomon Stubbing, gardener.
Agreement for taking care of the garden

To provide 30 loads of dung to be spread a year
To scour ditches, watercourses, maintain paths, lawns, clip hedges, prune trees, shrubs, and vines
Maintain all hothouses, frames and tools

He could pasture one horse free

Inventory of goods included

Nine, three light frames, glazed	A wine sieve	One, two light framed, glazed
Two setts	One, one light frame, glazed	A dutch hoe
Eleven bell glasses	Three nine wick hoes	One grind stone and trough
Two small hoes	Two water barrows and tubs compleat	One drill hoe
Three wheel barrows	Three dung forks	Two iron reels and lines
Two scythes and sheaths	Three iron teeth garden rakes	One watering pot
Three pairs of garden shears	One pail, one trowel	Four stools
One iron bowl	Two hundred and forty earthen garden pots of different sizes	
Ten mortis locks and two keys	Four step ladders	

signed by Solomon Stubbing [who could write well]

Valuation of Crops at Gidea Hall 1 October. 1793 £16. 15s. 6d.

A piece of white broccoli plant	A piece autumn spinach small
A piece cabbages stumps	15 beds carrot
A piece autumn cauliflower	A piece small turnips,
2 beds scorzenera north side wall	A large piece savoy red cabbage amongst artichoke
A piece purple broccoli	15 short rows french beans for seed
13 beds onions, very thin crops	A large piece of cabbage stalks and red cabbage
11 rows small celery	All the edging parsley
1 bed red beetroot	All the endive autumn cauliflower under south wall
15 rows celery	All the endive, lettuce, horseradish, french beans
6 seed beds broccoli, savoys, cafe	Cauliflower plants in the melon ground
2 beds small leeks	All the horseradish north side wall
9 beds parsnips north side wall	2 beds salsify north side wall

BIBLIOGRAPHY

General

Carter, G., Goodes, P., and Kedrin L. Humphry Repton, Landscape Gardener 1752-1818. 1982

Hadfield, Miles. A History of British Gardening. 1979

Hunter, J. The Essex Landscape. 1999

Prince, H. Parks in England. 1967

Stroud, D. Humphry Repton. 1962

Audley End

Cowell, F. Richard Woods, ?1716-1783, A Preliminary Account. [Garden History Spring 1987, Vol. 15 n l.]

Addison, William. Audley End. 1953

Player, J. Sketches of Saffron Walden, 1845

Williams. J. D. Audley End: The Restoration of 1762-1797. 1966

E.R.O., T/Z 75/13 A study of the work of Robert Adam and 'Capability' Brown at Audley End for Sir John Griffin Griffin.

Ibid., T/B 125/7, before 1600

Ibid., T/M 172, 1666

Ibid., D/DBy A24/10

Ibid., DDBY Pl, c.1750

Ibid., D/DQy 8, 1783

Ibid., D/DQy 20, c.1828

Barrington Hall

Galpin, Rev. F. W. The household expenses of Sir Thomas Barrington. ' [E.A. T. N.S. xii. 203]

Galpin, Rev. Canon F. W. 'The household expenses of Sir John Barrington, 1645-1667' [E.A.T. N.S. xxiii. 280]

V.C.H. viii. 167

E.R.O., D/DQ 14/38, 1766

Belhus

Barrett-Lennard, T. An Account of the Families of Lennard and Barrett. 1908

Cowell, F. op. cit.

Merton, A. R., 'Belhus, Aveley', [Essex Journal, vi. 51]

Sparkes Ivan. G., Belhus and the Barrett-Lennard family, 1964

Tipping, H. A. 'Belhus' [Country Life, xlvii. 656. 690]

V.C.H. viii. 6.

E.R.O., D/DL Z28 p22.

Ibid., D/DL Pl. 1619

Ibid., D/DL P2 Mr. Driver's sketch for a garden at Belhouse 1765.

Ibid., D/DL M14, Survey of manor of Belhus, 1619

Birch Hall

E.R.O., D/DR F67,69

Ibid., D/DE1 P22, 1800

Boreham House

Bryant, M. E., 'Boreham House' [Essex Review, lvi. 204]

Cowell, F. op. cit.

E.R.O., D/CT 40, 1838

Ibid., D/DGe P35, c.1840

Bower House

E.R.O., T/Z 31 Works of Charles Bridgeman

V.C.H. vii. 10

Braxted Park

E.R.O., T/M 415, c.1740

Ibid., T/M 423, 1822

Ibid., T/M 426, 1831

Ibid., D/CT 48, 1839

Brizes

Cowell, F., op cit.

E.R.O. D/Dro P1, 1788

Claybury

Essex Review xxxvii. 102 quoting E.R.O. D/DQs 25

E.R.O., T/Z 13/50 Some Essex Works of Humphry Repton

Lockwood, H. H., 'Claybury and the Survival of the Golden Woods.' [Essex Heritage ed .K. Neale]

V.C.H. v. 195.

Copford Hall

Harrison, A.D., 'Manor of Copford Hall', [E.A.T. N.S. xxii. 355]

E.R.O., D/DE1 P73, 1845

Ibid., D/DE1 P32, 1817

Ibid., D/DU 588/2/1-16

Ibid., T/M 282, 1784

Copped Hall

Cassidy, R. Copped Hall, a short history. 1983

Cassidy, R. Copped Hall in its heyday. 1986

Farmer, J. The Great Copped Hall fire. 1993
Steegman, J. The artist and the country house. 1949
V.C.H. v. 118
'Copped Hall' Country Life. xxviii. 610,646 Oct/Nov. 1910
E.R.O., D/DW E28/8,9, 36/1
Ibid., D/DW E30/2, c.1750
Ibid., T/M 125, c.1590

Danbury Park
Powell, W.R. 'John Round of Danbury Park' [Essex Heritage ed. K. Neale]
Clay, H. 'Danbury Park' [Essex Review xxvii. 17]
Hopkirk, M. Danbury, Historical notes and records of the village of Danbury. 1945
E.R.O., Sale Cat. B13, 1892
Ibid., D/DMa P8, 1758

Down Hall
Willis, P. 'A poet's gardener'. The Listener 24 Dec. 1964
V.C.H. viii. 169
E.R.O., T/Z 31 Works of Charles Bridgeman.

Easton Lodge
Spurrier, Felice. The Maynards of Easton Lodge. 1987
Gordon G. 'Lady Warwick's Garden', The Gardener's Magazine, 2 Mar. 1907.
Edwards, P. 'Underneath the arches, pergolas and arbours in classical tradition' Country Life clxix, 720, 19 Mar. 1981
Plumptre, G. The Garden Makers,' The great tradition of Garden Design from 1600 to the present day.
E.R.O., D/DMg E23 Lutyens plans for cottages, 1900
Ibid., D/DMg Pl Map of Manor of Little Easton, 1730

Gidea Hall
Drury, John Treasures of Havering. 1998
Sparkes, Ivan G. Gidea Hall and Gidea Park. 1966
E.R.O., D/DBe E4
Ibid., D/DQb Pl Romford, 1807

Glazenwood
Smith, C. Fell 'Glazenwood', Essex Review xliii. 24
D.N.B.
Leaflet from owners

Gosfield Hall
Gorton, P. & Bates, L. M. The Story of Gosfield Hall. 1988
Barr, G. Gosfield Hall, a short history. 1961
Beckett, J. V. 'Gosfield Hall: a country estate and its owners, 1715-18251 [Essex Archaeological Transactions xxv [1994], 185.]

Hallingbury Place
Cocks, Heather M. E. M The great house of Hallingbury: its place in history. 1988
Country Life 19 Sept. 1914
V.C.H. viii. 117

Hatfield Priory
Cowell, F. op. cit.

Ham House
Hingston Fox, Dr. R. Dr. John Fothergill and his friends. 1919
Sainsbury, Frank. 'Ham House Estate, Upton, West Ham and its people'. [Essex Heritage ed. K. Neale]
Dunning, B. 'American who changed English Gardens' [Country Life 8 Sept. 1966]
D.N.B. Fothergill

Highams
V.C.H. vi. 260

Hill Hall
Dewar, M. Sir Thomas Smith: A Tudor intellectual in office. 1964
Neale, Kenneth. 'Sir Thomas Smith and Hill Hall'. [Essex Journal v.1970, l.]
V.C.H. iv. 281.

Hylands House
Foreman Stephen. Hylands, the story of an Essex country house and its owners.2nd ed. 1999
Abraham, E. Hylands, an architectural history. 1988
E.R.O. D/DAn Pl
Ingatestone Hall
Emmison, F. G. Tudor Food and Pastimes. 1964
Emmison, F. G. Tudor Secretary: Sir William Petre at Court and Home. 1961
Edwards, A. C. John Petre. 1975
Yearsley, Ian. Ingatestone and Fryerning. 1997
E.R.O., D/DP All

Ibid., D/DP Pl, Ingatestone Hall, 1566

Leyton Grange
V.C.H . vi.186

Langleys
Steer, F. W. Samuel Tufnell of Langleys, 1682-1758. 1960
E.R.O., D/DTu 276
Ibid., T/Z 31

Marks Hall
Ryan, M. A History of Marks Hall. 1994
Marks Hall Estate and arboretum, an introduction. [visitors' centre leaflet]
'Marks Hall, the seat of Mr. T. P. Price.' Country Life, xi. 144. 1 Feb. 1902
Country Life, 29 Sept. 1923
Essex Countryside, Vol. 39 No. 415, July 1991
E.R.O., D/DCm P14, 1764
Ibid., D/CT 234 Tithe Map
Ibid., Sale Cat. B2311, 1897

Moor Hall
E.R.O., D/DEs T6
V.C.H., viii. 139

Moulsham Hall
Edwards, A. C. The Account books of Benjamin Mildmay, Earl Fitzwalter. 1977
Grieve, H. The Sleepers and the Shadows, Vol. II. 1994
Jeffers, R. H. 'Moulsham Hall, Chelmsford 1729-1809' [Essex Journal Vol. IV 7-8]

New Hall, Boreham
Sier, L.C. 'New Hall Park'. [Essex Archaeological Transactions N.S. xiv. 96.]
Cowell, F. 'Richard Woods 1716-93 A Preliminary Account.' [Garden History Autumn 1986 Vol. 14 n 2.]
Country Life, 24 Oct. 1914

Rivenhall Place
Loudon, J.C. The Landscape Gardening and Landscape Architecture of the late Humphry Repton, Esq. 1840
Wicks, G. 'Raising of a Country House'. [Essex Countryside Dec. 1990 vol. 409 no. 408].

E.R.O., D/DFg Pl/18, 1716-7
Ibid., D/DFg P9, c.1825

Shortgrove Hall
Hanson M. 'Phoenix to arise by the Granta' [Country Life 9 Apr. 1981]
E.R.O., D/DU 205/19 Widdington, 1786
Ibid., T/M 298 Widdington map, 1727
Spains Hall
Freeman, E. The Ruggles Family of Spains Hall, Finchingfield, Essex. 1993
Haslam, R. 'Spains Hall, Essex'. [Country Life 11 Jan. 1902, 6 Jan. 1983 and 30 Dec. 1982]
Ruggles-Brise, Colonel Sir John. Spains Hall, Finchingfield. [A short history written by the owner]

St. Osyth's Priory
Walker, K. & Titmarsh, H. St. Osyth's Priory, Past, Present and Future
Tipping, H. A. English Homes ii, 271
Astbury, A. 'St Osyth Priory' [Country Homes Oct. 1909]
E.R.O., D/DU 268/15, 1762

Stansted Hall
E.R.O., T/A 229

Stubbers
V.C.H. vii. 113
'History over the Garden Wall' [Essex Countryside May 1990]
Ramsbottom, J. 'Old Essex Gardeners and their Gardens' [Essex Naturalist xxvi. 65]
Hadfield, Miles. A History of British Gardening, 1979
Russell, J. M. 'Stubbers, North Ockenden'. [Essex Archaeological Transactions N.S. xxi. 47]
E.R.O., T/A 598/1

Thorndon Hall
Edwards, A. C. John Petre. 1975
Chambers, D.C. The planters of the English Landscape. 1993
Tooby, J. The Early Introduction of Camellias to England from China. 1981
Dunning, B. 'American who changed English Gardens'. [Country Life 8 Sept. 1966]
'The Death and Fame of Robert James, 8th Lord Petre.' [Essex Journal Vol. 5, 1970. 56]

Ward, J. Old Thorndon Hall. 1972
Clutton, Sir G. 'The Gardeners of the Eighth Lord Petre'. [Essex Naturalist xxxii. 201]
Clutton, Sir G. & Mackay, C. 'Old Thorndon Hall, Essex: a History and Reconstruction of its Park and Garden.' [Garden History Society Occ. Papers No. 2, 1970]
Grieve, H. E. P. A Transatlantic Gardening Friendship, 1981
E.R.O., D/DP P5, 1598
Ibid., D/DP P23/1, 1733
Ibid., D/DP P30, 1778
Ibid., D/DP P41, 1805
Ibid., D/DP P43, 1808

Wanstead House
Addison, William. Wanstead Park. c.1973
Dawson, O. S. The Story of Wanstead Park. c.1894
Eastment, Winifred. Wanstead Through the Ages. 1969
Dunlop, I & Kimball, F. 'The Gardens of Wanstead House, Essex'. [Country Life, 28 July 1950]
V.C.H. Essex, vi. 324
E.R.O., D/DB P35, c.1725
Ibid., D/DCw P7, c.1725
Ibid., D/DCw P20, 1813
Ibid., D/DCw P35, 1811
Ibid., D/DCw P37, c.1850
Ibid., D/DCw P42, 1819
Ibid., D/DCw P59, 1779
Ibid., D/DCw P61, c.1825
Ibid., D/DP P32, 1712

Warley Place
Le Lièvre, Audrey. Miss Willmott of Warley Place: her life and her gardens. 1980
Sedgewick, M. R., Russell, P. and Rolt, D. "Memories of Miss Ellen Willmott 1858-1934" The Garden, R.H.S. Journal Aug. 1976
Harper, G. Warley Magna to Great Warley. 1984
Herring, I. J. 'The Great Gardener of Great Warley'. [Essex Countryside Nov. 1969]
Stearn, W. T. 'Ellen Willmott gardener and botanical rosarian'. The Garden R.H.S. Journal. June 1979
Shenstone, J.C. 'The Gardens of Warley Place, Brentwood. [Essex Naturalist xvii.)
Willmott, Ellen. Warley Garden in Spring and Summer, 1909
E.R.O., Sale Catalogues, B2, 1875, B1318 and B921, both 1935
Ibid., T/Z 147/1,4,6

Wivenhoe Park
Butler, N. The Story of Wivenhoe, 1989
Cowell, F. op. cit.
Feesey, R. A History of Wivenhoe Park, 1963
E.R.O., D/DHt Bl
Ibid., D/DMb P4, 1827
Ibid., T/M 271, 1765
Ibid., T/M 275, c.1840

Woodford Hall
E.R.O. T/B 92, 1801

INDEX